No greater sacrifice

No greater sacrifice

The Atonement and Redemption of Christ

Steven L. Shields

INTERNATIONAL STANDARD BOOK NUMBER
0-88290-166-4

LIBRARY OF CONGRESS CATALOG CARD NUMBER
80-83864

Printed and Distributed in the
United States of America
by

**Horizon
Publishers &
Distributors**

P.O. Box 490
50 South 500 West
Bountiful, Utah 84010

"Greater love hath no man than this, that a man lay down his life for his friends."

JOHN 15:13

To The Reader

This work has been prepared to bring together, in one volume, some of the more important teachings of Latter-day Saint leaders concerning the mission and atonement of the Savior. These men have pondered deeply the meanings of Christ's redemptive acts and the Saints are able to draw great benefit from their insights and understandings.

Since many of the sermons referred to herein touched on more than one aspect of the gospel, only those parts specifically pertaining to the topic of this book have been included. We have not endeavored to provide interpretations; this is left to the reader.

Considerable effort has been expended to assure that the quotations included in this book have been accurately recorded. In all cases, references have been provided, and the following abbreviations have been used:

CR—*Conference Reports*
JD—*Journal of Discourses*
Scriptural references are those commonly used.

The compiler's contribution to this work has been four-fold. First, choosing the key articles from those which were available; second, selecting the parts of those articles most pertinent to the subject at hand; third, adding sub-titles and highlighting key thoughts to make the work more useable and fourth, providing a comprehensive index.

In each article or discourse cited, the compiler has added subtitles and has indicated major insights and contributions in italicized type.

Contents

The Sacrifice

Symbols of the Atonement

The Greatest Story in History

Introduction

The most important event ever to occur is the atonement of our Lord Jesus Christ. Without it, we are nothing and our lives on earth are in vain. It is because of His great sacrifice that each of us is able to obtain forgiveness of our sins and once again take our place in the celestial abode of our Father in Heaven.

We know from the scriptures that before this world was created, our Elder Brother offered himself as the sacrifice of sacrifices. He proposed free agency, a great blessing, in order that we might learn and experience the difference between good and evil, and choose for ourselves. For this reason we have the opportunty of becoming like God and of becoming one with God.

In the Book of Mormon, we have the first recorded instance of the Savior appearing to a mortal being, more than 2,000 years before His own birth. On this special occasion, he told the brother of Jared, "Behold, I am he who was prepared from the foundation of the world to redeem my people. Behold, I am Jesus Christ. I am the Father and the Son. In me shall all mankind have light, and that eternally, even they who shall believe on my name; and they shall become my sons and my daughters. (Ether 3:14)

We are told in other passages that the sacrifices which were performed in Old Testament times under the Law of Moses were a symbolic representation of the final sacrifice of the Savior. Adam, in his obedient innocence, was asked by an angel as to his purpose in offering sacrifices. He replied that he did it because he had been commanded to do so. The Angel then taught Adam this principle, ". . . This thing is a similitude of the sacrifice of the Only Begotten of the Father, which is full of grace and truth." (Moses 5:7)

The limitless love our Father in Heaven has for us is incomprehensible. For a father to even ponder the thought of allowing his son to sacrifice himself for his brothers and sisters is tremendous. The love our brother Jesus Christ has for us, to step boldly forward and declare, "Here am I, send me," is indescribable.

Imagine, if you will, the agony of that final night in Gethsemane, when our Savior ". . . kneeled down, and prayed, saying, Father, if thou be willing, remove this cup from me: nevertheless not my will, but thine, be done. And there appeared an angel unto him from heaven, strenthening him. And being in agony he prayed more earnestly: and his sweat was as it were great drops of blood falling to the ground." (Luke 22:41-44)

The agony of our own sins, no matter how small they may be, can sink us to the very depths of despair. It is impossible to imagine what the sins of the whole world—past, present and future—would feel like. The torture Christ experienced must have been excruciating. Of that heavy burden He has told us: "For behold, I God, have suffered these things for all, that they might not suffer if they would repent; but if they would not repent they must suffer even as I; which suffering caused myself, even God, the greatest of all, to tremble because of pain, and to bleed at every pore, and to suffer both body and spirit—and would that I might not drink the bitter cup, and shrink—nevertheless, glory be to the Father, and I partook and finished my preparations unto the children of men." (D&C 19:16-19)

As we share the insight and wisdom of the inspired men of God contained herein, let us remember that "God so loved the world, that he gave his only begotten Son, that whosoever believeth in him should not perish, but have everlasting life." (John 3:16)

Truly, there could be no greater sacrifice.

The Plan

"He will swallow up death in victory; and the Lord God will wipe away tears from off all faces . . ." (Isaiah 25:8)

The Plan of Redemption

This article is probably the first published statement by the Church on this topic, outside of scriptural record. Although the author is unknown, it has been assumed that the statement originated with the First Presidency of the Church. It appeared in print in the March, 1834 issue of the Evening and Morning Star, *the official Church newspaper.*

God Has Influenced Man for Good

It is reasonable to suppose, that *man departed from the first teachings, or instructions which he received from heaven in the first age, and refused by his disobedience to be governed by them.* Consequently, he formed such laws as best suited his own mind, or as he supposed, best adapted to his situation. But that *God has influenced man more or less since that time in the formation of law for his benefit* we have no hesitancy in believing; for, as before remarked, he being the source of all good, every just and equitable law was in a greater or less degree influenced by him.

Man Instructed to Form Wise Laws

And though man in his own supposed wisdom would not admit the influence of a power superior to his own, yet for wise and great purposes, for the good and happiness of his creatures, *God has instructed man to form wise and wholesome laws, since he had departed from him and refused to be governed by those laws which he had given by his own voice from on high in the beginning.*

Plan of Redemption Prepared Before the Fall of Adam

But notwithstanding this transgression, by which man had cut himself off from an immediate intercourse with his Maker without a Mediator, it appears that *the great and glorious plan of his redemption was previously meditated; the sacrifice prepared; the atonement wrought out in the mind and purpose of God,* even in the person of the Son, through whom man was now to look for acceptance, and through whose merits he was now taught that he alone could find redemption, since the word had been pronounced, "Unto dust thou shalt return."

But that *man was not sufficient of himself to erect a system, or plan with power sufficient to free him from a destruction which awaited him,* is evident from the fact that God, as before remarked, prepared a sacrifice in the gift of his own Son which should be sent in due time, in his own wisdom, to prepare a way, or open a door through which man might enter into his presence, from whence he had been cast for disobedience.

From time to time these glad tidings were sounded in the ears of men in different ages of the world down to the time of his coming. By faith in this atonement or plan of redemption, Abel offered to God a sacrifice that was accepted, which was the firstlings of the flock. Cain offered of the fruit of the ground, and was not accepted, because he could not do it in faith: he could have no faith, or could not exercise faith contrary to the plan of heaven.

Blood of Christ Must Be Shed

It must be the shedding of the blood of the Only Begotten to atone for man; for this was the plan of redemption; and without the shedding of blood was no remission; and as the sacrifice was instituted for a type, by which man was to discern the great sacrifice which God had prepared; to offer a sacrifice contrary to that, no faith could be exercised, because redemption was not purchased in that way, nor the power of atonement instituted after that order; consequently, Cain could have no faith: and *whatsoever is not of faith is sin.* But Abel offered an acceptable sacrifice, by which he obtained witness that he was righteous, God testifying of his gifts. Certainly the shedding of the blood of a beast could be beneficial to no man, except it was done in imitation, or as a type, or explanation of what was to be offered through the gift of God himself; and this performance done with an eye looking forward in faith on the power of that great sacrifice for the remission of sins.

Abel Was Instructed in The Plan of Redemption

But however various may have been, and may be at the present time the opinions of men respecting the conduct of Abel, and the knowledge which he had on the subject of atonement, it is evident in our minds, that he was instructed more fully into the plan than what the Bible speaks; for how could he offer a sacrifice in faith, looking to God for a remission of his sins in the power of the great atonement, without having been previously instructed into that plan? And further, if he was accepted of God, what were the ordinances performed further than the offering of the firstlings of the flock?

God Delivered The Whole Plan Of the Gospel to Abel

It is said by Paul in his letter to his Hebrew brethren, that *Abel obtained witness that he was righteous, God testifying of his gifts.* To whom did God testify of the gifts of Abel, was it to Paul? We have very little on this important subject in the fore part of the Bible. But it is said, that Abel himself obtained witness that he was righteous. Then certainly God spoke to him: indeed, it is said that God talked with him; and if he did, would he not, seeing he was righteous, deliver to him the whole plan of the gospel? And is not the gospel the news of redemption? How could Abel offer a sacrifice and look forward with faith on the Son of God for a remission of his sins, and not understand the gospel?

Sacrifice Was Performed in Faith

The mere shedding the blood of beasts or offering anything else in sacrifice, *could not procure a remission of sins, except it were performed in faith of something to come,* if it could, Cain's offering must have been as good as Abel's. And if Abel was taught of the coming of the Son of God, was he not taught of his ordinances? We all admit that the gospel has ordinances, and if so, had it not always ordinances, and were not its ordinances always the same? Perhaps, our friends will say, that the gospel and its ordinances were not known till the days of John the son of Zecharias, in the days of Herod the king of Judea. But we will here look at this point: For our own part, we cannot believe, that the ancients in all ages were so ignorant of the system of heaven as many suppose, since all that were ever saved, were saved through the power of this great plan of redemption, as much so before the coming of Christ as since; if not, God has had different plans in operation, (if we may so express it,) to bring men back to dwell with himself; and this we cannot believe, since there has been no change in the constitution of man since he fell; and *the ordinance or institution of offering blood in sacrifice, was only designed to be performed till Christ was offered up and shed his blood, as said before, that man might look forward with faith to that time.* (*The Evening and Morning Star*, Vol. II, No. 18, Kirtland, Ohio, March, 1834, pg. 143)

Salvation—The Mission of Jesus Christ

Joseph F. Smith

This discourse was delivered by President Joseph F. Smith in the Tabernacle in Salt Lake City on Sunday, June 18, 1882. At the time he was a counselor to President John Taylor.

Man, Both Mortal and Immortal

We are called mortal beings because in us are the seeds of death, but in reality we are immortal beings because there is also within us the germ of eternal life.

Man is a dual being, composed of the spirit which gives life, force, intelligence and capacity to man, and the body which is the tenement of the spirit and is suited to its form, adapted to its necessities, and acts in harmony with and to its utmost capacity yields obedience to the will of the spirit. The two combined constitute the soul. The body is dependent upon the spirit, and the spirit during its natural occupancy of the body is subject to the laws which apply to and govern it in the mortal state.

Temporal and Spiritual Death

In this natural body are the seeds of weakness and decay, which, when fully ripened or untimely plucked up, in the language of scripture is called "the temporal death." The spirit is also subject to what is termed in the scriptures and revelations from God, "spiritual death." The same as that which befell our first parents, when *through disobedience and transgression, they became subject to the will of Satan and were thrust out from the presence of the Lord and became spiritually dead, which the Lord says, "is the first death,* even that same death which is the last death, which is spiritual, which shall be pronounced upon the wicked when I shall say, Depart, ye cursed!" And the Lord further says, "But, behold I say unto you, that I the Lord God gave unto Adam and unto his seed, that they should not die as to the temporal death until I the Lord

God should send forth angels to declare unto them repentance and redemption (from the first death) through faith on the name of mine only begotten Son. And thus did I, the Lord God, appoint unto man the days of his probation, that by his natural death he might be raised in immortality unto eternal life, even as many as would believe, and they that believe not unto eternal damnation, for they cannot be redeemed from their spiritual fall because they repent not."

Redemption Through Faith in Christ

From the natural death, that is the death of the body, and also from the first death, "which is spiritual" there is redemption through belief on the name of the "only Begotten Son," in connection with repentance and obedience to the ordinances of the Gospel, declared by holy angels, for *if one "believes," he must also obey;* but from the "second death," even that same death which is the first death, "which is spiritual," and from which man may be redeemed through faith and obedience, and which will again be pronounced upon the wicked when God shall say, "depart ye cursed," there is no redemption, so far as light on this matter has been revealed.

All Sin But Blasphemy Against the Holy Ghost May Be Forgiven

It is written that "all manner of sin and blasphemy shall be forgiven unto men who receive me and repent; but the blasphemy against the Holy Ghost, it shall not be forgiven unto men." *If men will not repent and come unto Christ, through the ordinances of His Gospel, they cannot be redeemed from their spiritual fall, but must remain forever subject to the will of Satan and the consequent spiritual darkness or death into which our first parents fell,* subjecting all their posterity thereto, and from which none can be redeemed but by belief or faith on the name of the "only begotten Son" and obedience to the laws of God.

Provisions of The Gospel Are Merciful

But, thanks be to the Eternal Father, through the merciful provisions of the Gospel all mankind will have the opportunity of escape or deliverance from this spiritual death either in time or in eternity, for not until they are freed from the first can they become subject unto the second death, still if they repent not "they cannot be redeemed from their spiritual fall," and will continue subject to the will of Satan, the first spiritual death, so long as "they repent not."

Who Are Sons of Perdition?

I have been speaking of those who repent not, and thereby reject Christ and His Gospel, but what of those who do believe, repent of their sins, obey the Gospel, enter into its covenants, receive the keys of the Priesthood and the knowledge of the truth by revelation and the gift of the Holy Ghost, and afterwards turn away wholly from that light and knowledge? They "become a law unto themselves," and "will to abide in sin," of such it is written, *"Whoso breaketh this covenant after he hath received it, and altogether turneth therefrom shall not have forgiveness in this world nor in the world to come."* And again—"Thus saith the Lord concerning all those who know my power and who have been made partakers thereof, and suffered themselves, through the power of the devil to be overcome and to deny the truth and defy my power—*they are they who are the sons of perdition of whom I say that it had been better for them never to have been born, for they are vessels of wrath doomed to suffer the wrath of God with the devil and his angels in eternity; concerning whom I have said there is no forgiveness in this world nor in the world to come;* having denied the Holy Spirit after having received it, and having denied the only Begotten Son of the Father, having crucified him unto themselves and put him unto an open shame."

Sons of Perdition Are Different From Others Who Reject the Gospel

Now, there is a difference between this class and those who simply repent not and reject the gospel in the flesh. Of these latter it is written, "they shall be brought forth by the resurrection of the dead through the triumph and the glory of the Lamb," and "shall be redeemed in the due time of the Lord after the sufferings of His wrath." But of the others it is said, "they shall not be redeemed," for "they are the only ones on whom the second death shall have any power." The others never having been redeemed from the first, cannot be doomed to the second death, or in other words, cannot be made to suffer eternally the wrath of God, without hope of redemption through repentance, but must continue to suffer the first death until they repent, and are redeemed therefrom through the power of the atonement and the Gospel of salvation, thereby being brought to the possession of all the keys and blessings to which they will be capable of attaining or to which they may be entitled, through the mercy, justice and power of the ever-living God, or on the other hand forever remain bound in the chains of spiritual darkness, bondage and banishment from his presence, kingdom and glory.

Spirit Is Eternal

The "temporal death" is one thing, and the "spiritual death" is another thing. The body may be dissolved and become extinct as an organism, although the elements of which it is composed are indestructible or eternal, but I hold it as self-evident that the spiritual organism is an eternal, immortal being, destined to enjoy eternal happiness and a fullness of joy, or suffer the wrath of God, and misery—a just condemnation, eternally. *Adam became spiritually dead, yet he lived to endure it until freed therefrom by the power of the atonement, through repentance, etc. Those upon whom the second death shall fall, will live to suffer and endure it, but without hope or redemption.* The death of the body or natural death is but a temporary circumstance to which all were subjected through the fall and from which all will be restored or resurrected by the power of God, through the atonement of Christ.

Man existed before he came to this earth, and he will exist after he passed from it; and will continue to live throughout the countless ages of eternity.

Man Exists in Three Different Conditions

There are three classes of beings, or rather man exists in three separate conditions before and after his probation upon this earth—first in the spirit or pre-existent state, second in the disembodied state, the condition which exists after the dissolution of the body and spirit until the resurrection take place, and third in the resurrected state. For instance, *some fourteen hundred years before the coming of Christ into the world to sojourn in the flesh, he showed himself to the brother of Jared and said, "Behold, this body, which ye now behold, is the body of my spirit, and man have I created after the body of my spirit; and even as I appear unto thee to be in the spirit, will I appear unto my people in the flesh."*

Christ Was Prepared From the Foundation Of the World

He further declared, "Behold I am he who was prepared from the foundation of the world to redeem my people. Behold I am Jesus Christ." Here "Jesus showed himself unto this man in the spirit, even as he shewed himself unto the Nephites"—that is prior to his coming in the flesh. This I consider typical of the first condition of all spirits. Again it is written, *"for Christ also hath once suffered for sins, the just for the unjust, that he might bring us to God,* being put to death in the flesh, but quickened by the spirit, by which also he went and preached unto the spirits in prison, which sometime were disobedient, when once the longsuffering of God waited in the days of Noah, while the ark was in preparation wherein few, that is eight souls, were saved by water," etc. Thus we see that while the body of our Savior slept in the tomb, He went in the spirit, and preached his glorious Gospel to "the spirits in prison," who were disobedient in the days of Noah, and were destroyed in the flesh by the flood. This was their second condition or state in the spirit awaiting the resurrection of their bodies which were slumbering in death. "Marvel not at this," saith Jesus, "for the hour is coming in the which all that are in their graves shall hear his (the Redeemer's) voice and shall come forth, they that have done evil unto the resurrection of damnation." In reference to the third condition or state we will refer to the account given of the risen Redeemer before his ascension.

Condition of Resurrected Beings

John tells us that he appeared unto his disciples three times after his resurrection, on which occasions he ate bread, broiled fish and honeycomb, and opened the eyes of their understanding, that they began to comprehend the Scriptures and the prophecies concerning Christ. But when he appeared unto them "they were terrified and affrighted and supposed that they had seen a spirit. And he said unto them, Why are ye troubled? And why do thoughts arise in your hearts? *Behold my hands and my feet that it is I myself; handle me and see me; for a spirit hath not flesh and bones as ye see me have." Here is presented the true type of the resurrected being.* And after this manner are all those who have their resurrected bodies, and there are many of these, for we are told in the scriptures, that, "the graves were opened, and many bodies of the Saints which slept arose and came out of the graves, after his resurrection, and went into the holy city and appeared unto many." This class of beings dwell in heaven, or in the paradise of the just, having been counted worthy to come forth in the first resurrection, even with Christ, to dwell with him and to be associates with and members of the kingdom of God and his Christ. These comprise the three conditions or estates of man in heaven.

Not All Enjoy the Same Privileges

Not all, however, of the disembodied spirits enjoy the same privileges, exaltation and glory. The spirits of the wicked, disobedient, and unbelieving are denied the privileges, joy and glory of the spirits of the just and the good. *The bodies of the Saints will come forth in the first resurrection, and those of the unbelieving, etc., in the second or last. In other words, the Saints will rise first, and those who are not Saints will not rise until afterwards, according to the wisdom, justice and mercy of God.*

Christ is The Great Example

Christ is the great example for all mankind, and I believe that mankind were as much foreordained to become like him, as that he was foreordained to be the Redeemer of man. Whom God did foreknow—and whom did he not foreknow? "He also did predestinate to be conformed to the image of His Son, that He might be the firstborn among many brethren." It is very plain, that mankind are very far from being like Christ, as the world is today, only in form of person. In this we are like him, or in the form of his person, as he is the express image of His father's person. *We are therefore in the form of God, physically, and may become like him in the possession of knowledge, intelligence, wisdom and power.*

The grand object of our coming to this earth is that we may become like Christ, for if we are not like him, we cannot become the sons of God, and be joint heirs with Christ.

Righteous Who Are Resurrected Are Greater Than Angels

The man who passes through this probation, and is faithful, being redeemed from sin by the blood of Christ, through the ordinances of the Gospel, and attains to exaltation in the kingdom of God, is not less but greater than the angels, and if you doubt it, read your Bible, for there it is written that the Saints shall "judge angels," and also they shall "judge the world." And why? *Because the resurrected, righteous man has progressed beyond the pre-existent or disembodied spirits, and has risen above them, having both spirit and body as Christ has, having gained the victory over death and the grave, and having power over sin and Satan, in fact having passed from the condition of the angel to that of a God.* He possesses the keys of power, dominion and glory that the angel does not possess—and cannot possess without gaining them in the same way that he gained them, which will be by passing through the same ordeals and proving equally faithful. It was so ordained when the morning stars sang together, before the foundations of this earth were laid. *Man in his pre-existent condition is not perfect, neither is he in the disembodied state. There is no perfect estate but that of the risen Redeemer, which is God's estate, and no man can become perfect except he becomes like them.*

The Nature of God

And what are they like? I have shown what Christ is like, and he is like his Father, but I will refer to an undoubted authority to this people, on this point, "The Father has a body of flesh and bones as tangible as man's, the Son also, but the Holy Ghost has not a body of flesh and bones, but is a personage of spirit; were it not so the Holy Ghost could not dwell in us." (Doc. and Cov., Sec. 130) There is not time to refer to the many scriptural passages which might be cited in proof of these important facts, enough already has been referred to, to place the matter beyond a doubt.

Savior's Mission on Earth Not Completed Until After the Resurrection

It is believed by many in the Christian world, that our Savior finished his mission when he expired upon the cross, and his last words on the cross, as given by the Apostle John—"It is finished," are frequently quoted as evidence of the fact; but this is an error *Christ did not complete his mission upon the earth until after his body was raised from the dead.* Had his mission been completed when he died, his disciples would have continued fishermen, carpenters, etc., for they returned to their several occupations soon after the crucifixion, not yet knowing the force of their holy calling, nor understanding the mission assigned them by their Master, whose name would soon have been buried with his body in the grave to perish and be forgotten, "for as yet they knew not the scripture that He must rise again from the dead." But the most glorious part of his mission had to be accomplished after the crucifixion and death of his body. When on the first day of the week some of the disciples went to the tomb with certain preparations for the body of their Lord, they were met there by two men clothed in "shining garments," who said unto them, "Why seek ye the living among the dead? He is not here but is risen. Remember how He spoke unto you when He was yet in Galilee, saying the Son of Man must be delivered into the hands of sinful men and be crucified, and the third day rise again." And not until then did the disciples remember these words of the Savior, or begin to understand their meaning. Why were they thus forgetful, and seemingly ignorant of all they had been taught by the Savior respecting the objects of his mission to the earth? Because they lacked one important qualification, they had not yet been "endowed with power from on high." They had not yet obtained the gift of the Holy Ghost. And the presumption is, they never would have received this important and essential endowment had Christ's mission been completed at the time of his death. It may seem strange to some who may not have reflected on this matter fully, that the disciples of Christ were without the gift of the Holy Ghost until after his resurrection. But so it is written, notwithstanding the Savior on one occasion declared, "blessed art thou Simon, etc., for flesh and blood hath not revealed this unto thee, but my Father which is in heaven." *While Jesus was with them he was their light and their inspiration.* They followed him by sight, and felt the majestic power of his presence, and when these were gone they returned to their nets and to their various occupations and to their homes saying, "we trusted that it had been he which should have redeemed Israel, but the chief priests and our rulers have delivered him to be condemned to death, and have crucified him." No wonder that Jesus exclaimed unto some of them, "O fools, and slow of heart to believe all that the Prophets have written."

The Disciples Receive the Holy Ghost

If the Disciples had been endowed with the "gift of the Holy Ghost," or "with power from on high," at this time, their course would have been altogether different from this as the sequel abundantly proved. If Peter, who was the chief Apostle had received the gift of the Holy Ghost, and the power and testimony thereof prior to the terrible night on which he cursed and swore and denied his Lord, the result would have been different with him, for then he would have sinned against "light and knowledge," and "against the Holy Ghost," for which there is no forgiveness. The fact, therefore, that he was forgiven, after bitter tears of repentance, is an evidence that he was without the witness of the Holy Ghost, never having received it. The other disciples or apostles of Christ were precisely in the same condition, and *it was not until the evening of the day on which Jesus came out of the grave, that he bestowed upon them this inestimable gift.* John gives a careful description of this important event which concludes as follows: "Then said Jesus to them again, Peace be unto you; as my Father sent me, even so send I you. And when he had said this he breathed on them and said unto them, Receive ye the Holy Ghost, whosoever sins ye remit, they are remitted unto them," etc. This was their glorious commission, and now were they prepared to receive the witness of the Spirit—even the testimony of Jesus Christ. Yet they were told to "tarry in Jerusalem until they were endued with power from on high," which they did. Jesus further told them that if he went not away the "Comforter"—that is the Holy Ghost—would not come unto them, but if he went away he would "send him," and he it was who should testify of Christ, and of the Father, and bring to their remembrance "all things whatsoever" he had commanded or taught them, and it should "lead them into all truth." Thus we see that the resurrection from the dead, not only of Christ but of all mankind, in the due time of the Lord; the endowment of the Apostles with the Holy Ghost, and their glorious commission from Christ, being sent out by him as he was sent by the Father; the opening of the eyes of the disciples to understand the prophecies of the Scriptures, and many other things did Jesus after he cried out upon the cross, "It is finished." *Further, the mission of Jesus will be unfinished until he redeems the whole human family, except the sons of perdition, and also this earth from the curse that is upon it, and both the earth and its inhabitants can be presented to the Father redeemed, sanctified and glorious.* *(JD 23:169-175)*

The Gospel Plan

Charles W. Penrose

At the time he delivered this sermon, Elder Penrose was serving as the editor of the Deseret News, *the official Church newspaper in the Salt Lake area. He gave this address to the congregation assembled in the Assembly Hall in Salt Lake City, April 25, 1880. A number of years later, Elder Penrose was called as an Apostle, and then into the First Presidency of the Church.*

Simple Belief in Christ Is Not Enough for Exaltation

The Latter-day Saints are often accused by the people in the Christian world of being very much deluded. Our religion is counted a delusion and a snare. I was thinking, however, during the meeting this afternoon about the great number of Christian preachers who today are standing up in various parts of the world informing the people who listen to them that simple belief on the Lord Jesus, who died on Calvary, is all that is necessary to save them and exalt them in the presence of God the Father. And it seems to me that if there is one delusion more pernicious than another it is that very doctrine, which seems to be a fundamental principle of all the various Christian sects. You will find, go where you will in the Christian world and listen to any of the great preachers of the day, that this is the common topic of discourse. Jesus Christ is preached—which is quite right, I am very glad that he is—as the Savior of the World.

So we testify as Latter-day Saints. In connection, however, with this great truth which is proclaimed to the inhabitants of the earth by men professing to be sent of God, is preached the great error that mere belief in the work which Jesus Christ wrought out is sufficient for the salvation of the people. The inhabitants of the earth are informed that it is not by any works of righteousness which they may perform that they can gain any favor whatever in the sight of God, but it is the righteousness of Christ alone which is acceptable to the Father and which they can gain the benefit of if they simply believe in him.

When we search the Scriptures and read the sayings of Jesus Christ, and of his servants whom he sent forth to preach the Gospel, we do not find any such statement as this. We find, it is true, that the apostles of the Lord Jesus preached Christ and him crucified to the world wherever they had an opportunity; they directed the attention of the people, Jew and Gentile, wherever they went, to Jesus of Nazareth who was slain on Calvary as the Redeemer of the world, and faith in him was declared to be absolutely necessary.

Commandments Must Be Obeyed to Obtain Salvation

But we do not find that in proclaiming faith in the Lord Jesus Christ to that generation they informed the people that a mere belief in Christ was all that was needful; we find that, in addition to teaching the principle of faith in God and in his Son Jesus Christ, they taught the people it was necessary to observe certain rules, and commandments, to obey certain forms and ordinances, to comply with certain conditions that they might obtain the benefit of the shedding of Christ's blood. We find by searching the New Testament, which contains some of the teachings of the apostles and some of their letters to the churches, that the doctrine was held forth by them that "the blood of Christ cleanseth us from all sin." We find that this applied, as they taught it, not only to what is called original sin, but also to actual sin.

Original Sin Versus Actual Sin

The sin which our first parents committed in the Garden of Eden is called original sin; and the sins committed individually by the inhabitants of the earth, are called actual sin, for "all have sinned and come short of the glory of God." The apostles sent forth to preach the Gospel by our Savior himself, taught the people that *through the shedding of Christ's blood remission of sin might come to all and that mankind might be redeemed from sin, original and actual.* But we find this distinction in their teaching in regard to original sin, and their teaching in regard to individual sin; that the blood of Christ redeems mankind from the effects of the fall and will eventually bring up all who died in Adam—for "as in Adam all die, even so in Christ shall all be made alive,"—but that while people had nothing whatever to do with the sin which Adam committed and therefore have nothing whatever to do with the work of atonement for that sin, yet for their own sins there is some action required on their part that they may obtain redemption therefrom, inasmuch as the blood of Christ was shed for original sin unconditionally, but for the remission of actual sin conditionally.

Adam's Fall Introduced Death Into the World

God, when he placed our first parents in the Garden of Eden put before them a certain tree, the fruit of which he said "they should not partake of, if they did they should surely die." They partook of that tree in disobedience to the divine commandment, and planted the seeds of death in their bodies, and that death has passed upon all their posterity. "It is appointed unto men once to die." *This act of our first parents introduced death into the world. Death came by sin, and death has passed upon all the posterity of Adam and Eve.*

Jesus Is Called the Second Adam

Jesus came in the meridian of time as "the Lamb of God which taketh away the sin of the world," to bring mankind up from the effects of the transgression of our first parents. Hence, he is called "the Second Adam," and we are told that as in the first Adam all die, even so in Christ, the second Adam, shall all be made alive again. And he himself proclaimed that the time should come, "in the which all that are in the graves shall hear the voice of the Son of God and shall come forth; they that have done good, unto the resurrection of life; and they that have done evil unto the resurrection of damnation," or in the words of the inspired translation, "they that have done good in the resurrection of the just, and they that have done evil in the resurrection of the unjust." *It is through the transgression of Adam that we have to suffer what is called the temporal death.* Through that transgression our spirits have become separated from our bodies; our immortal spirits held by these mortal tabernacles must be taken out, and our bodies must return to the ground and crumble into dust; *but by the atonement wrought out by the Lord Jesus Christ the time is to come when all who lived in the body shall live in the body again.*

Christ Opened The First Resurrection

Christ was raised from the dead and became "the first fruits of them that slept;" afterwards they that are Christ's at his coming will be brought forth. This is the first resurrection. "Blessed and holy," says the Apostle John in his vision, "are they that hath part in the first resurrection; on such the second death hath no power, but they shall be priests of God and of his Christ, and shall reign with him a thousand years." After that John saw that "the sea gave up the dead which were in it; and death and hell delivered up the dead which were in them; and they were judged every man according to his works."

Christ Atoned For The Original Sin

The atonement wrought out by the Lord Jesus Christ for original sin will apply just as far as the effects of the sin are felt. *As all the posterity of Adam died through that sin, even so all the posterity of Adam will be raised up again through the atonement.* "But every man in his own order," says the apostle, "Christ the first fruits; afterward they that are Christ's at his coming;" and then after the thousand years have passed away, the rest of the dead, as John said, will be brought forth and judged each one according to the deeds done in the flesh.

Free Agency—We Are Accountable to God

All must give an account unto the great eternal Father. We are responsible for the acts done in the flesh, for like as it was in the case of our first parents, good and evil, truth and error, are placed before us, and every individual is left free to choose the good and refuse the evil, or to choose the evil, and refuse the good as he pleases. Both are set before us and, if we yield to either it will lead us in either direction.

The Light of Christ Leads All Men to God

There is, however, a spirit in man, born in him, which comes from God, the fountain of light and truth. This light is planted in the breast of every man and every woman who breathes the breath of life. It is the true light that lighteth every man that cometh into the world, and *if people would listen to the whispering of that still small voice, be led by that natural light and natural inspiration, they would be led up to God.* By this natural light, by this general inspiration, if people would listen to its whisperings, and be guided thereby, they would be led up to the fountain of light. "Every good gift," says the Apostle James, "and every perfect gift is from above, and cometh down from the Father of light in whom there is no variableness neither shadow or turning." *But on the other hand there must be, as the Book of Mormon says, "an opposition in all things,"* and there is a spirit of evil, a spirit of darkness, which draws downward to earth, and a spirit of light which leads upward to life; the one leads to Satan and his works, the other to God and to righteousness. But the inhabitants of the earth generally have been more prone to listen to the inspiration of the spirit of darkness as did our first parents, than to listen to the still small voice of light and life in their souls.

All Are Held Accountable In Varying Degrees

All people must give an account of the deeds done in the body according to the measure of light they have received, and the opportunities they have had of obtaining that light, while they dwelt in the flesh. Some people have lived on the earth when God has sent his servants inspired of him to make plain his ways, while others have tabernacled in the flesh when no inspired voice was heard, when no communication was open between the heavens and the earth. And he who is just, who is the embodiment of the eternal principles of justice, will deal out to all according to their light and according to the opportunities they have had of obtaining that light, but all must be judged, all must appear before the judgement seat of Christ and give an account for their individual works.

"Modern" Gospel Differs From the Gospel of Christ

Now, we will take the case of an individual who has broken all the laws of God and perhaps all the laws of man, and finally has shed the blood of a fellow-creature, and is condemned by the laws of man to die; he is, in fact, unfit to live, unfit to associate with mortal beings, therefore, they must needs thrust him out of the world that he may mingle with immortal beings. Where do they send him to? A minister will come and preach to him, and tell him that all he has to do is cast his soul on Jesus; that he has just to believe that Christ died for him, and the righteousness of the pure, immaculate, sinless Christ will be grafted into that rotten branch, so that he will have the fruits of righteousness and peace. That is according to the modern Gospel. The man believes this, he confesses Christ with his lips and acknowledges him with his tongue, and straightway is strung up between the heavens and the earth, and choked to death; his spirit is forced out of his body, and ushered into the presence of the eternal Father to stand before his spotless throne, and is deemed fit to dwell in the society of the pure and holy ones on high. That is according to the modern Gospel, but not according to the ancient Gospel of Jesus Christ, the everlasting Gospel which says "no murderer hath eternal life abiding in him."

Only One Way to Obtain Forgiveness

But some one may ask, "Is there no efficacy, for actual sin, in the atonement wrought out by Jesus Christ? Is there no method by which people can obtain a forgiveness of their individual sins?" *Yes, there is a way, and that is the plan of the true Gospel, but it does not consist in mere belief in the righteousness of another;* mere belief in the righteousness of somebody else will not make us any better ourselves. What is to be done then? Here the Gospel is very plain and simple, when pointed out by one who understands it. But "how shall they call on him in whom they have not believed? And how shall they believe in him of whom they have not heard, and how shall they hear without a preacher, and how shall they preach except they be sent?" It is men who are not sent who preach the nonsense we hear in the world. It is men who are not sent who deceive mankind with their strong delusions, and then turn round and call the Latter-day Saints deluded. If they were sent of God they would not preach such nonsense, they would not deceive mankind and thus become the cause of so much sin and evil in the world. For while people believe that at the last moment, at the last gasp of their existence, they may cast their souls on Jesus, and by believing in his virtue escape the penalty of their sins, they will continue to sin on, like many of these false teachers who revel in sin up to their very eyes, and will die in their sins and go down into the pit where they must wait until they are released, in the time and way of the Lord.

Belief in Christ is But The Foundation

The doctrine of belief without works is a strong delusion. *There is more to do, according to the Gospel, than merely to believe in the Lord Jesus Christ.* Belief in the Lord Jesus Christ is necessary. That is the foundation, it is the root of the matter, but it is not all the matter. "Believe on the Lord Jesus Christ and thou shalt be saved." Why? Because *if you have true faith in Christ, if you really believe on him, you will believe in his sayings and keep his commandments.* Hear him: "If ye love me, keep my commandments." *"Not every one that saith Lord, Lord shall enter into the kingdom of heaven; but he that doeth the will of my Father which is in heaven."* "Therefore, whosoever heareth these sayings of mine, and doeth them, I will liken him unto a wise man which built his house upon a rock: And the rain descended and the floods came, and the winds blew, and beat upon that house; and it fell not; for it was founded upon a rock. And every one that heareth these sayings of mine, and doeth them not, shall be likened unto a foolish man which built his house upon the sand: And the rain descended and the floods came, and the winds blew, and it fell; and great was the fall of it."

The Holy Ghost to Guide Men to Truth

When Jesus Christ sent his apostles unto all the world after he had risen from the dead, he commanded them to "teach all nations baptizing them in the name of the Father, and of the Son and of the Holy Ghost. Teaching them to observe all things whatsoever I have commanded you." They were to go out and preach to all the world, baptising those that believed, and then proceed to teach all things whatsoever he had commanded them. Christ taught his disciples many principles while he tarried with them in the flesh, and after he had risen from the dead he continued his instructions from time to time. He also told them that when he went away the Comforter should come to reveal unto them the things of the Father and the Son, and to guide them unto all truth; for it is only by receiving truth and living it that people can be saved and exalted. "Sanctify them through thy truth," prayed the Savior, "thy word is truth." The Holy Ghost, the Comforter, was to come, therefore, to make plain the truth, and to reveal things past, present, and to come.

Every Blessing to Man Comes Through Christ

It is necessary, however, to have faith in Christ. Why? Because every blessing that flows to the inhabitants of the earth from God the eternal Father comes through Jesus Christ. We must first of all believe in God, then believe in Jesus Christ, and *if we really do believe in God and in Jesus Christ, and the desire will enter our hearts to turn away from sin.* Thus it is said, "whosoever heareth these sayings, and doeth them, I will liken unto a wise man, which built his house upon a rock." It is taught by some that repentance is the first principle of religion, but if a man does not believe in God, will he pray unto him? What has a man to repent of except the breaking of the commandments of God? And how shall he feel anything to repent of if he does not believe in God? It is necessary therefore to have faith first, and then comes repentance, a determination to forsake evil, and this is what the ancient apostles taught.

Baptism Symbolic of The Death and Resurrection of Christ

What next? We find that wherever the apostles went, whenever they found a people who believed in Jesus and repented of their sins they baptized them. By sprinkling a little water in their face? Or by making the sign of the cross upon their foreheads? No. *They were taken down into the water and buried there in the likeness of Christ's death and burial and raised up in the likeness of his resurrection, that henceforth having "put off the old man with his deeds" they might walk in newness of life,* observe his laws and keep his commandments, and follow his footsteps, for he "left us an example, that we should follow in his steps." Then the apostles laid their hands upon those that were baptized, and we read that they received the Holy Ghost, the Comforter, the spirit of truth, which opened up a communication between each individual soul and the fountain of light and eternal truth, which testified that they had been washed clean from their sins. How washed? By water? Yes and no. *Water does not wash away sin, but if people desire remission of their actual sins they must be baptized.* Thus it must be, "to fulfill all righteousness." *Even Christ himself had to be baptized to fulfill that commandment, and if he had not obeyed it there would have been no manifestation of the Holy Ghost resting upon him in the sign of a dove, and a voice from heaven, declaring, "This is my beloved Son in whom I am well pleased."* Christ left us his example, and his apostles followed in his footsteps, baptising according to the commandment for the remission of sins. John the Baptist also taught this same doctrine when he went out to preach in Judea, and when the people came to him confessing their sins he baptized them in Jordan for the remission of sins. "I indeed baptize you," says John, "with water; but one mightier than I cometh, the latchet of whose shoes I am not worthy to loose; he shall baptize you with the Holy Ghost and with fire."

Baptism for the remission of sins! "Why," says one "I thought the blood of Christ redeemed us from our sins." And so it does. Water itself will not wash away guilt. If a person has no faith in Christ, and has not repented of his sins, baptism will be of no avail. But baptism properly administered by one who has a right to administer in the name of the Father, and of the Son, and of the Holy Ghost, will avail. The person to be baptized must go down into the water and therein be buried for a remission of sins, having repented, and having faith in the Lord Jesus Christ and in his atoning blood, for *the blood of Christ was shed "for the sins of the whole world." But the "whole world" will not receive the benefit of the atonement unless they comply with the conditions laid down, namely: faith, repentance, and baptism.* They who do not receive this ordinance cannot enter into the presence of the Father, for "except a man be born of water and of the spirit, he cannot enter into the kingdom of God." *(JD 21:80-86)*

To Overcome Death

John Taylor

John Taylor was President of the Church during the years 1880 to 1887. His book, "The Mediation and Atonement," was published in 1882. It is a volume which beautifully explains the topic, and is the source for this selection.

Death Is Overcome Through the Atonement

In the economy of God and the plan proposed by the Almighty, it is provided that man was to be placed under a law apparently simple in itself, yet the test of that law was fraught with the gravest consequences. The observance of that law would secure eternal life, and the penalty for the violation of that law was death. For, we are told, in Adam all die, and hence the declaration, *"It is appointed for man once to die."* There is another principle associated with this, which is, that *the atonement provided a means and plan whereby death could be overcome,* and the resurrection of the body from death be brought about, for it is written, "As in Adam all die, even so in Christ shall all be made alive." But without this atonement the resurrection of the body could not be brought about; hence Jesus, when on earth, proclaimed, "I am the Resurrection and the Life," and He Himself "was the first fruits of them that slept."

Breaking God's Law Had a Purpose in the Eternal Plan

Men could not have been tested without a law. The penalty for the violation of that law was death. *If the law had not been broken, man would have lived; but would man thus living have been capable of perpetuating his species, and of thus fulfilling the designs of God in preparing tabernacles for the spirits which had been created in the spirit world?* And further, could they have had the need of a mediator, who was to act as a propitiation for the violation of this law, which it would appear from the circumstances was destined to be broken; or could the eternal increase and perpetuity of man have been continued, and his high exaltation to the Godhead been accomplished, without the propitiatory atonement and sacrifice of the Son of God?

Jesus said, "Thus it is written, and thus it behooved Christ to suffer." Could it have behooved Christ to suffer if man had not sinned, and was it not part of the eternal plan of God that man should violate that law, that an atonement might be provided and had, and by this means man be purified and perfected, through the struggles and trials incident to his coming in contact with the powers of darkness, and, through the mediation and atonement of Jesus Christ, and his own obedience to the requirements of the law associated therewith, be raised to a higher state of existence than it would have been possible for him to have obtained without the transgression of that law?

Adam Learned the Purpose of Sacrifice from an Angel

These points are made exceedingly plain in the Pearl of Great Price. It is there stated:

"And Adam called upon the name of the Lord, and Eve also, his wife; and they heard the voice of the Lord from the way towards the garden of Eden, speaking unto them, and they saw him not; for they were shut out from his presence. And he gave unto them commandments, that they should worship the Lord their God, and should offer the firstlings of their flocks, for an offering unto the Lord. And Adam was obedient unto the commandments of the Lord. And after many days an angel of the Lord appeared unto Adam, saying, Why dost thou offer sacrifices unto the Lord? And Adam said unto him, I know not, save the Lord commanded me. And then the angel spake saying, *This thing is a similitude of the sacrifice of the Only Begotten of the Father,* which is full of grace and truth. Wherefore, thou shalt do all that thou doest in the name of the Son, and thou shalt repent and call upon God in the name of the Son for evermore. And in that day the Holy Ghost fell upon Adam, which beareth record of the Father and the Son, saying, I am the Only Begotten of the Father from the beginning, henceforth and for ever, that as thou hast fallen thou mayest be redeemed; and all mankind, even as many as will. And in that day Adam blessed God and was filled, and began to prophesy concerning all the families of the earth, saying, Blessed be the name of God, for because of my transgression my eyes are opened, and in this life I shall have joy, and again in the flesh I shall see God. And Eve, his wife, heard all these things and was glad, saying, *Were it not for our transgression we never should have had seed, and never should have known good and evil, and the joy of our redemption, and the eternal life which God giveth unto all the obedient.* And Adam and Eve blessed the name of God; and they made all things known unto their sons and their daughters."

Adam and Eve Gained Through the Fall

Thus we find: Firstly. That Adam and Eve both considered that they had gained, instead of suffered loss, through their disobedience to that law; for they made the statement, that if it had not been for their transgression they never would "have known good and evil." And again, they would have been incapable of increase; and without that increase the designs of God in relation to the formation of the earth and man could not have been accomplished; for *one great object of the creation of the world was the propagation of the human species, that bodies might be prepared for those spirits who already existed, and who, when they saw the earth formed, shouted for joy.*

Secondly. By pursuing the course they did, through the atonement, they would see God as they had done before; and furthermore, they would be capable of exaltation, which was made possible only through their fall, and the atonement of Jesus Christ; and also, they might have the comforting influence of the Spirit of God, and His guidance and direction here, as well as eternal lives and exaltations in the world to come.

Paul, in his Epistle to the Romans, also writes very directly upon these truths; he says:

"Nevertheless, death reigned from Adam to Moses, even over them that had not sinned after the similitude of Adam's transgression, who is the figure of him that was to come. But not as the offense, so also is the free gift. For if, through the offense of one many be dead, much more the grace of God, and the gift of grace, which is by one man, Jesus Christ, hath abounded unto many. And not as it was by one that sinned, so is the gift; for the judgment was by one to condemnation, but the free gift is of many offenses unto justification. *For if by one man's offense death reigned by one; much more they which receive abundance of grace and of the gift of righteousness shall reign in life by one Jesus Christ.* Therefore, as by the offense of one judgment came upon all men to condemnation; even so by the righteousness of one the free gift came upon all men unto justification of life. For as by one man's disobedience many were made sinners, so by the obedience of one shall many be made righteous. Moreover, the law entered, that the offense might abound. But where sin abounded, grace did much more abound:

that as sin hath reigned unto death, even so might grace reign through righteousness unto eternal life, by Jesus Christ our Lord." (Romans 5:14-21)

Adam Fell that Men Might Be

Whilst in the Book of Mormon Lehi teaches:

"And now, behold, if Adam had not transgressed, he would not have fallen; but he would have remained in the garden of Eden. And all things which were created, must have remained in the same state which they were, after they were created; and they must have remained for ever, and had no end. And they would have had no children; wherefore, they would have remained in a state of innocence, having no joy, for they knew no misery; doing no good, for they knew no sin. But behold, all things have been done in the wisdom of Him who knoweth all things. Adam fell that men might be; and men are, that they might have joy. And the Messiah cometh in the fulness of time, that he may redeem the children of men from the fall. And because that they are redeemed from the fall, they have become free for ever, knowing good from evil; to act for themselves, and not to be acted upon, save it be by the punishment of the law at the great and last day, according to the commandments which God hath given. Wherefore, men are free according to the flesh; and all things are given them which are expedient unto man. And they are free to choose liberty and eternal life, through the great mediation of all men, or to choose captivity and death, according to the captivity and power of the devil; for he seeketh that all men might be miserable, like unto himself." (2 Nephi 2:22-27)

In the same book it is written:

"Yea, I know that ye know, that in the body he shall show himself unto those at Jerusalem, from whence we came; for it is expedient that it should be among them; for it behooveth the great Creator that he suffereth himself to become subject unto man in the flesh, and die for all men, that all men might become subject to him. For as death hath passed upon all men, to fulfil the merciful plan of the great Creator, there must needs be a power of resurrection, and the resurrection must needs come unto man by reason of the fall; and the fall came by reason of transgression; and because man became fallen, they were cut off from the presence of the Lord. Wherefore it must needs be an infinite atonement. Save it should be an infinite atonement, this corruption could not put on incorruption. Wherefore, the first judgement which came upon man must needs have remained to an endless duration. And if so, this flesh must have laid down to rot and to crumble to its mother earth, to rise no more. O the wisdom of God! his mercy and grace! For behold, if the flesh should rise no more, our spirits must become subject to that angel who fell from before the presence of the eternal God, and became the devil, to rise no more." (2 Nephi 9:5-8)

There is a principle developed in the above quotation to the effect that death was "passed upon all men to fulfil the merciful plan of the great Creator; and furthermore, that the resurrection came "by reason of the fall." *For if man had not sinned, there would have been no death and if Jesus had not atoned for the sin, there would have been no resurrection.* Hence these things are spoken of as being according to the merciful plan of God. This corruption could not have put on incorruption, and this mortality could not have put on immortality; for as we have elsewhere shown, men by reason of anything that he himself could do or accomplish, could only exalt himself to the dignity and capability of man and therefore it needed the atonement of a God, before a man, through the adoption could be exalted to the Godhead.

Again, if the body could not have been resurrected, it would have had to "crumble to its mother earth," and remain in that condition of ascending to the Godhead; and furthermore, not only would our bodies have lost their entity, their life and power, but the spirit also would have been placed in a state of subjection "to that angel who fell before the presence of the eternal God, and became the devil," without a capability of even hope of life, salvation, and exaltation, and would have been deprived of all free agency and power, and subject to the influences, dominion and eternal destruction of Lucifer, the enemy of man and of God.

Lucifer's Plan was to Do Away With the Atonement

Hence, on this ground, and because of the terrible effects which would have resulted to humanity from the proposed plan to deprive man of his free agency, and in seeking to do away with the atonement, Lucifer was cast out of heaven, as were also those associated with him in the same diabolical plans and purposes.

The testimony of the Book of Doctrine and Covenants is in full accord with the revelations in the ancient scriptures. In it we are instructed that God "created man, male and female, after his own image and in his own likeness created he them, and gave unto them commandments that they should love and serve him, the only true God and that he should be the only being whom they should worship. But by the transgression of these holy laws, man became sensual and devilish, and became fallen man. *Wherefore the Al-*

mighty God gave his Only Begotten Son, as it is written in those scriptures which have been given of him. *He suffered temptations, but gave no heed unto them; he was crucified, died, and rose again the third day; and ascended into heaven, to sit down on the right hand of the Father, to reign with almighty power according to the will of the Father."* (D&C 20:18-24)

God's Commandments are Spiritual

Again, we read from the same source:

"Behold, I gave unto him that he should be an agent unto himself: and I gave unto him commandment, but no temporal commandment gave I unto him, for my commandments are spiritual, they are not natural, neither carnal nor sensual." (D&C 29:35)

"Wherefore, it came to pass that the devil tempted Adam, and he partook the forbidden fruit and transgressed the commandment, wherein he became subject to the will of the devil, because he yielded unto temptation. Wherefore, I the Lord God caused that he should be cast out from the garden of Eden, from my presence, because of his transgression, wherein he became spiritually dead, which is the first death, even that same death, which is the last death, which is spiritual, which shall be pronounced upon the wicked when I shall say, Depart, ye cursed. But, behold, I say unto you, that I the Lord God gave unto Adam and to his seed that they should not die as to the temporal death, until I the Lord God should send forth angels to declare unto them repentance and redemption, through faith on the name of mine Only Begotten Son. And thus did I, the Lord God, appoint unto man the days of his probation; that by his natural death he might be raised in immortality unto eternal life, even as many as would believe. (D&C 29:40-43)

In accordance with this we find it written in the Pearl of Great Price, that the Lord did send an angel to Adam (as elsewhere quoted) who taught unto him the Gospel.

Thus it would appear that if any of the links of this great chain had been broken, it would have interfered with the comprehensive plan of the Almighty pertaining to the salvation and eternal exaltations of those spirits who were His sons and for whom principally the world was made; that they through submission to the requirements of the eternal principle and law governing these matters might possess bodies and these bodies united with the spirits might become living souls, and being the sons of God, and made in the image of God, they, through the atonement might be exalted by obedience to the law of the Gospel; to the Godhead.

(John Taylor, The Mediation and Atonement, 1882, pp. 128-135)

Because Man Has Sinned

Orson Pratt

Elder Orson Pratt, a member of the Quorum of Twelve Apostles from the early days of the Church, was called upon to deliver this funeral sermon during memorial services for the Honorable Leonidas Shaver. Judge Shaver was the judge of the First Judicial District Court of the United States, in and for the Territory of Utah. The services were held in the Council House in Salt Lake City, June 30, 1855.

Man Sinned—Death Resulted

It is a decree of Jehovah who governs and controls the destinies of worlds, who controls all intelligent beings, that man should die. No one can escape this decree! No one can prevail with the grim monster death, and overcome him, but we must sooner or later meet that enemy of mankind, and be laid prostrate in the tomb.

Why is it that so great and good a Being, a Being who is full of benevolence and love, a Being who is filled with mercy and compassion, should suffer such a dire calamity to befall the human race? Why is it? Is it because He delights in the sufferings of mankind? Is it because he delights to see them writhe in pain and distress? No: it is because man has sinned; it is because he has offended his Maker—because he has transgressed sacred and holy laws, because he has subjected himself to the monster death, to the miseries, wretchedness, and vanities of this life. *It is not, however, because we ourselves have sinned that death comes upon us; but it is because of the original sin;* for all will admit that infants that are incapable of sinning against God, who are unacquainted with His revealed will, who discern not between good and evil, fall victims to the destroyer, as well as others. If, then, this curse seizes upon the innocent and upon those who have not transgressed the laws of heaven, it must be in consequence of the original sin that so great a calamity is in the world.

Resurrection Is A Free Gift

"By man came death." says the Apostle Paul. Again the same Apostle says, "As by the offence of one judgment came upon all men to condemnation; even so by the righteousness of one the free gift came upon all men unto justification of life." (Rom. 5:18) What free gift? *The free gift of salvation from the grave, the salvation of our bodies,* or in other words, of our corporeal systems. The redemption of our bodies from the grave is brought about through the atonement of Jesus Christ; *hence we have had no agency in bringing death into our world, and we have no agency in the redemption of our world. One man brought death into the world, and one man brought redemption from death.*

Death Affects All—Redemption Affects All

This redemption is just as extensive as the curse, so far as the body is concerned. The curse affected all, and the bodies of all will be redeemed. When I speak of this redemption, I wish to be distinctly understood, that I mean the redemption of the body from the grave. If the fall lays all mankind low in the dust, the redemption will bring them forth from the dust. If the fall shut them out from His face and presence, the redemption will bring them back into His presence to behold His face.

Jesus was lifted up by sinful man upon the cross; what for? That all mankind might be lifted up from the grave to be judged before God; not for Adam's sins, but for their own personal sins; hence there is no person dwelling upon the face of the earth that is free from the original curse that came in consequence of the transgression of Adam.

If we had no sins of our own, we should ever remain, after this universal redemption of our bodies, in the presence of God, but if we individually have committed sins, we shall be again cast out from the presence of God, unless we have complied with the great plan of salvation revealed by our Savior.

All Mankind Will Not Be Saved In the Presence of God

The great question raised by many with regard to the extent of the atonement, is, "Will all mankind be saved eternally in the presence of God, in the celestial kingdom, who have personally sinned?" No; they will not. *There is a certain class of mankind that will be saved in the fulness of celestial glory,* and partake of all the blessings held forth by the plan of redemption. *But this applies only to those who are faithful and obedient.*

There are others who will partake of a portion of this redemption; but they will differ from the first, as much as the moon differs from that bright luminary of heaven—the sun. Hence Paul, in speaking of the redemption of man, says there are bodies celestial, and bodies terrestrial, and the glory of the celestial is one and that of the terrestrial another, and by the glory of the stars he represents a third class of beings. And again, in order to show the difference existing in this third class, he says, as one star differeth from another star in glory, so also is the resurrection of the dead.

(JD 2:368-369)

From The Beginning

John Taylor

President John Taylor delivered this discourse in Provo, Utah, Sunday, August 28, 1881.

God Knew That Man Would Fall

Was it known that man would fall? Yes. We are clearly told that it was understood that man should fall, and it was understood that the penalty of departing from the law would be death, death temporal. And there was a provision made for that. Man was not able to make that provision himself, and hence we are told that it needed the atonement of a God to accomplish this purpose; and the Son of God presented himself to carry out that object. And when he presented himself for this position he was accepted by His Father, just the same as any man who owes a debt, if he is not able to pay that obligation, and somebody steps forward and says, I will go security for him. If the persons to whom he is indebted are willing to take him as security they will receive the security's note or obligation to meet the debt. So Jesus offered himself. Now, man could not have done that. Man could do all that he is capable of doing.

An Eternal Law Was Violated

But there was an eternal law of God violated and *it needed an eternal infinite sacrifice to atone therefor;* and Jesus offered himself as that sacrifice to atone for the sins of the world; and hence it is written, *he was the Lamb slain from before the foundation of the world.*

Now, to carry out this view of indebtedness a little further. We will suppose that a man was given his note to pay a certain amount in a certain given time, and in order to keep that note good, he agrees to pay interest on it. Now, when Jesus gave himself up as security for the sins of mankind, and God accepted of his security, what was done then? Why, *sacrifices were introduced as types of the sacrifice of the Son of God,* to show that the ancient servants of God recognized this principle which had existed in the heavens and many of them understood the principle with great clearness.

Adam Offered Sacrifices in Faith

We find that Adam offered sacrifices, and when he did this, he said in answer to a question put to him by a holy angel, I do not know why I do it, only the Father has commanded it. And then the angel commenced to explain to him that the rite was a type of the sacrifice of the Only Begotten of the Father who should come in the meridian of time to offer himself as a sacrifice for the sins of the world; and said he, "Thou shalt do all things in the name of the Son, and call upon the Father in his name for evermore."

Adam Had to Fall in Order to Have Posterity

When Adam and Eve ate of the forbidden fruit, the mercy of God was extended to them, and they perceived as Eve expressed it, that if there had been no fall, they would have had no posterity, and that they would have been deprived of many joys and blessings relating both to this life and the life to come. And so Adam and Eve rejoiced in their hearts that God had provided the plan, and although they were fallen, yet in this life, through the atonement, they would have joy, and by and by they would return to their Father, and there rejoice exceedingly in the abundant mercy of God, and in the redemption wrought out for them by the Son of God. *(JD 22:300-301)*

A Plan of Mercy

Orson Pratt

Elder Orson Pratt, perhaps one of the most eloquent speakers in the Church during his lifetime, delivered many sermons on the topic of the atonement. The following was delivered in the Old Tabernacle in Salt Lake City, September 11, 1859.

Plan of Redemption Devised Before Adam was Placed in the Garden

Now let us take into consideration for a few moments the great plan which God devised before Adam was placed in the garden of Eden in order to redeem man. God, by his foreknowledge, beheld that man would fall from his first estate, by turning aside from his commandments-that he would bring upon himself an eternal death both of body and spirit. Now is the opportunity for mercy to step in. Justice had consigned them to eternal death and misery, and mercy could not step in without destroying the claims of justice, only upon certain conditions.

Demands of Justice Had to Be Satisfied

And what may be those conditions? Would God accept the sacrifice of a corrupted, sinful, degraded, fallen being as an atonement for his own sins? No; that would not satisfy the demands of justice. *God could not exhibit the attribute of mercy on any principle whatsoever, only for a sinless being to suffer in behalf of sinful man.* Inasmuch as the sin was against an infinite being—a transgression of a law issued by an infinite being, the atonement must be an infinite atonement. Hence God sent forth his only begotten Son in the meridian of time, who took upon himself the form of fallen man: this is, he entered into a tabernacle of flesh and bones, although he had not been guilty of the original sin. This he did voluntarily on his part.

"Whom Shall We Send?"

For the edification of the Saints, I will refer to a passage in the inspired translation of the book of Abraham, where we read that in the counsels of eternity, before the foundation of the world, the Lord devised the great plan of salvation. When he came to that part of it, in relation to the future redemption of man, which pertains to a sacrifice, he made an inquiry—"Whom shall we send?" He did not feel, as it were, willing to say to any one of the council, *You* are the person, and *you* must go and make this atonement: he did not seem willing to exercise this authority upon an innocent being, but looked around upon the assembly as though he would have some one to volunteer. *"And one answered like unto the Son of Man, Here am I; send me."* Here, then, was an offer on the part of the Son of God, the Firstborn—"I will go and redeem the human family upon the conditions that thou hast devised."

God's Infinite Mercy

But how could he go and redeem them? He could not redeem them, unless he suffered for them and in their behalf. The penalty of death had passed upon them. His father might have reasoned with him in words something like these:—If you, a pure and sinless being, my only begotten Son, are willing to go and take upon you the same kind of body that the fallen sons of men have taken upon themselves—a fallen body of flesh and bones, subject to pain, disease, sickness, temptation, and finally death, and offer yourself as a sacrifice, (although it is not required of you, for you have committed no sin that I should cause death to come on your body; yet if you do this voluntarily, and keep my commandments in all things, and not sin against me,) I will accept the sacrifice which you make in behalf of your younger brethren; and I will have mercy on them, otherwise no mercy can be shown to them: justice must have its full effect, and they must suffer eternal misery, being captive to that being whom they have consented to obey.

Here then, was the principle in which mercy could be made manifest in behalf of the fallen sons and daughters of men. *When could this principle of mercy begin to be exercised? Could it be exercised before the blood of the atonement was shed? Yes.* There was the free, voluntary offer of the Son of God to do all this work, and suffer and die for his brethren, before man was placed in the garden: hence, in the mind of God, it was just the same as though it had actually been fulfilled. *Therefore he is called a lamb slain, as it were, before the foundation of the world:* hence he could have mercy on Adam, on Enoch, on Noah, on Abraham, on the Prophets, and on the children of men while the earth should stand, because of that atonement that was to be made in the meridian of time.

All Will Benefit From The Atonement

But the great question for us to consider, on this occasion, is, in what way the fallen sons and daughters of men can be made partakers of the benefits of this atonement? Are they to be unconditionally redeemed by the blood of Christ? Is it to be done by free grace alone, without any works on the part of the creature? or are there required on the part of the man certain conditions by which the atoning blood of Christ can have effect upon him. I will answer this question. *The atonement of Jesus Christ redeems mankind, so far as the fall is concerned, unconditionally.* Now, I want you all to understand this clearly. There is no faith, repentance, baptism, or works of any kind required on the part of man to be redeemed from the fall, or from the sins committed by our first parents. *Not one of you are guilty because Adam and Eve sinned.* Did you eat the forbidden fruit? Were you there, on that occasion, to put forth your hand, and take of that fruit, and eat of it? The united response of all the world in this and all generations of man would be—"We were not there." *You are not condemned for a sin you did not commit.* Can you repent of something you never have done? I defy the whole world to repent of Adam's sin, for they never committed it. You did not exercise your agency on that occasion: why, then, not be redeemed from it without exercising your agency? Why not be redeemed by free grace alone, without works? Why be required to believe, repent, and be baptized for Adam's sin? It would be foolishness. The atonement of Jesus Christ will redeem every son and daughter of Adam from his day down to the end of the earth, so far as that sin is concerned.

All Little Children Are Innocent Before God

Hence, all little children have been redeemed from the fall, and are perfectly innocent and pure before God. The original sin is not imputed to them. Why? Because of the atonement. The atonement is just as broad as the original sin and the effects of it. *If the original sin extends its effects to the latest generations of Adam, so the atonement will extend its effects to all his posterity,* and redeem them from these consequences.

Each Person Will Be Restored to Immortality

But you may inquire, if we are to be redeemed from Adam's sin and its consequences, unconditionally, by the atonement, shall we not be restored into the condition Adam was in before he fell? I answer, You will be. What condition was he in? He was an immortal being and *you will be restored to immortality, whether you be Saints or sinners.* The decree has gone forth that every man is to be raised to immortality. Then you will be as Adam was in the garden of Eden before he fell.

All Will Be Permitted To Stand Before God For Judgment

Furthermore, Adam, before he fell, was in the presence of God, and could behold the face of his Maker, hear his voice, look upon his glory, behold his angels, and associate with those pure and holy beings. Will you be restored back to the presence of God? Yes, after the resurrection; for Jesus says, "If I be lifted up, I will draw all men unto me,"—that is, lift them up from their graves, and bring them into his presence, to stand before the bar of his judgment. What for? To be judged. For Adam's sin? No. We have nothing to do with that sin in the day of judgment; but we shall be brought before the bar of God, and be restored from the fall, with flesh and bones, but not blood, and be capable of enduring forever and ever; and there we shall behold the face of our God and of Jesus Christ, and the face of his angels, and be able to converse with them, and hear them converse, as Adam did before the fall. Is not this a complete restoration? Yes.

Every Man And Woman Has Committed Sin

Now I want to tell you of something that will come a little closer home than Adam's sin. Every man or woman upon the face of this globe, that has come to the years of understanding and accountability, has committed sin himself or herself. You have had commandments given to you as well as our first parents had. The holy law has issued from heaven to us, and penalties have been affixed. And when we come up to years of understanding and accountability, we transgress the holy law and commandment given us from heaven, even as Adam transgressed the first law in the garden of Eden.

Now, let us consider the consequence of this second transgression. God has given a law to the posterity of Adam, after coming to a knowledge of good and evil by the fall, that they should not do evil. If he has given a strict law that we shall not do evil, you may depend upon it he has affixed a strict penalty to it; for what would a law be good for without a penalty? What is the penalty? It is, that if the posterity of Adam shall do evil, they shall, after the resurrection, be banished again from the presence of God, and from the glory of his power; they shall endure the pains of the second death. *The violation of the first law given to Adam brought the first death, and the violation of the second law given to the posterity of Adam will bring the second death,* which is the penalty attached to it. How are we going to help ourselves? We have all sinned after we came to the years of accountability. When we were little children, we were perfectly pure, even as the angels of God; and of such, said Jesus, is the kingdom of heaven, being redeemed from the fall by the atonement.

Atonement Will Not Automatically Redeem Man From Actual Sin

But are we redeemed from our own actual sins? *We have used our agency in committing these actual sins, and we have no excuse to plead.* We could justly excuse ourselves in relation to the sin committed by Adam, but there is no excuse in relation to breaking these second commandments. We have violated them with our eyes open. Can we escape the penalty? Says one, There is the atonement. Yes, that is true; but will that have effect to redeem us from this second death and banishment unconditionally on our part? No. *If we are redeemed from this second penalty, it will be by exercising our agency—by complying with certain conditions. . . .*

Jesus Has Done His Part

You can save yourselves through the atonement, or let it alone. Jesus has done his part: he has died for us—has got the plan all laid; his blood has been shed, and he has suffered the pains of all the children of men, and in their behalf, if they will only accept the conditions.

Requirements of Salvation

What is the first condition required of the human family? It is to *believe in Jesus Christ as the true Redeemer,* and in his

Father as the true God. This condition stands before repentance, baptism, the sacrament, or keeping the Sabbath day holy; for no person can keep the Sabbath day holy until he complies with the Gospel. This faith or belief is the first principle of the Gospel. "He that believeth and is baptized shall be saved," says Jesus Christ; "and he that believeth not shall be damned."

. . . *Believe that Jesus is, and that he has atoned for the children of man; believe that without his death and sufferings there could have been no forgiveness of sins; believe that his is the only name given under heaven whereby mankind can be saved.*

(JD 7:255-260)

That Great Plan

Orson F. Whitney

Elder Whitney, a member of the Quorum of Twelve Apostles, delivered this address during the October 1913 General Conference of the Church in Salt Lake City. Elder Whitney was a brilliant writer, and was well-known for his poetry.

Redemption and Exaltation Are Different

There is nothing so important to me or to you or to any of the children of men, as that great plan of life and salvation, devised in the heavens and delivered to man upon the earth in a series of Gospel dispensations of which this is the last and greatest.

What is this plan? What does it contemplate? What is its nature and purpose? Paul, the apostle wrote: "I am not ashamed of the Gospel of Christ for it is the power of God unto salvation." He might have gone further had it been timely, and shown that the Gospel of Christ is also the power of God unto exaltation. *Exaltation is salvation added upon;* it is an extension of that idea or condition, just as salvation is an extension of redemption. *A soul may be redeemed,* that is, raised from the grave, *and yet condemned at the final judgment* for evil deeds done in the body; or a soul may be saved, and yet come short of the glory that constitutes exaltation.

The Purpose of The Gospel

The threefold purpose of the gospel is to redeem and save and glorify the children of God.

The word "gospel" comes from "godspell," an Anglo-Saxon term meaning God-story, or the story of God. It derives its significance from that great central idea of the Christian faith—the coming of God as the Son of God to redeem and save mankind. *Abinadi, the Nephite prophet, declared, hundreds of years before the birth of the Savior, that God himself would come down among the children of men and redeem His people:* "and because he dwelleth in flesh He shall be called the Son of God." He is the author of our salvation. He paid our debt; He took the world out of pawn, in which it had been placed by the transgression of our first parents, Adam and Eve.

And yet, through that transgression, and the consequent fall of man, God's purpose was accomplished, in the coming of a race of spirits to take upon themselves bodies, thus becoming souls, capable of endless increase and everlasting progression. *"Adam fell that man might be, and man is that he might have joy."*

Christ Had To Die

But there would be no joy, no progress—there would be no redemption, no salvation, no exaltation, had not Christ died, that man might live again. The action of our first parents brought death, eternal death, into the world—death of the body, death of the spirit, everlasting banishment from God's presence; and yet it had the great result of giving God's children the opportunities which this life affords for education and development.

But in order that the plan might be operative, the transgression turned to good effect. God's purpose carried out, and man saved and glorified, there had to be a ransom, a redemption; the scales of eternal justice had to be repoised, and right's equilibrium restored. *The life of a God was the price of the world's freedom,* and that price was paid by him who is called Jesus, the Nazarene, but who was and is no other than Jehovah, the God of Israel, who came unto His own, was rejected by them, was crucified at their instigation, and gave His life to redeem the world.

(CR October 1913, pp. 97-98)

The Mission

"For behold, this is my work and my glory—to bring to pass the immortality and eternal life of man." (Moses 1:39)

The Mission of Jesus Christ

Melvin J. Ballard

Elder Ballard was ordained an apostle January 17, 1919. He delivered this discourse to General Conference in Salt Lake City in October 1936.

A Sacred Mission

The Church of Jesus Christ of Latter-day Saints has a sacred mission to perform in the world. One of the most important features of that mission is to provide new witnesses to this doubtful and skeptical generation that *Jesus is indeed the Christ, the very Son of the living God,* who died for men and is still interested in them and presides under his Father over the destinies of this world. We proclaim with John that by him, as the Father's representative, was the world made. In the character of Jehovah before he dwelt among men in the flesh, he was the Spokesman of his Father, Elohim, delivering the commandments, inspiring the prophets and ultimately coming to dwell among men in the flesh, thereafter to be called Jesus Christ. He gave himself as a ransom to save the world and mankind; first, from the consequences of the fall which brought mortality and death. He brings us to immortal and eternal life. And through our obedience to his Gospel he redeems us from the consequences of our own sins.

Christ is The Savior Of All Men

But his interest in this world did not end when he had performed his great sacrifice. He is the Savior of all men, no matter where or when they have lived upon the earth. To his disciples at Jerusalem he said, *"And other sheep I have, which are not of this fold; them also I must bring, and they shall hear my voice; and there shall be one fold, and one shepherd."* (John 10:16) It is generally agreed now that when he spoke those words there was a mighty multitude of people living in this western world. He was their Savior and knew of their existence.

Christ Visited America After His Resurrection

Prominent among the witnesses this Church produces to support the testimony of the disciples at Jerusalem concerning Christ and his ministry is the testimony of a nation living upon this western hemisphere which was visited by him after his resurrection. Unto them he said, "Ye are the other sheep of whom I spake." Great destructions had occurred in this land at the crucifixion of Christ. The multitude who survived were standing about one of the temples marveling at the great changes which had taken place. The following account of this visit is recorded in the Book of Mormon, the Bible of America, Third Nephi, 11th chapter:

"And it came to pass that while they were thus conversing one with another, they heard a voice as if it came out of heaven; and they cast their eyes round about, for they understood not the voice which they heard; and it was not a harsh voice, neither was it a loud voice; nevertheless, and notwithstanding it being a small voice it did pierce them to the very soul, and did cause their hearts to burn.

"And it came to pass that again they heard the voice, and they understood it not.

"And again the third time they did hear the voice, and did open their ears to hear it; and their eyes were towards the sound thereof; and they did look steadfastly towards heaven, from whence the sound came.

"And behold, the third time they did understand the voice which they heard; and it said unto them:

"Behold my Beloved Son, in whom I am well pleased, in whom I have glorified my name—hear ye him.

"And it came to pass, as they understood they cast their eyes up again towards heaven; and behold, they saw a Man descending out of heaven; and he was clothed in a white robe; and he came down and stood in the midst of them; and the eyes of the whole multitude were turned upon him, and they durst not open their mouths, even one to another, and wist not what it meant, for they thought it was an angel that had appeared unto them.

"And it came to pass that he stretched forth his hand and spake unto the people, saying:

"Behold, I am Jesus Christ, whom the prophets testified shall come into the world.

"And behold, *I am the light and the life of the world; and I have drunk out of that bitter cup which the Father hath given me, and have glorified the Father in taking upon me the sins of the world, in the which I have suffered the will of the Father in all things from the beginning.*

"And it came to pass that when Jesus had spoken these words the whole multitude fell to the earth; for they remembered that it had been prophesied among them that Christ should show himself unto them after his ascension into heaven.

"And it came to pass that the Lord spake unto them saying:

"Arise and come forth unto me, that ye may thrust your hands into my side, and also that ye may feel the prints of the nails in my hands and in my feet, that ye may know that I am the God of Israel, and the God of the whole earth, and have been slain for the sins of the world.

"And it came to pass that the multitude went forth, and thrust their hands into his side, and did feel the prints of the nails in his hands and in his feet; and this they did do, going forth one by one until they had all gone forth, and did see with their eyes and did feel with their hands, and did know of a surety and did bear record, that it was he, of whom it was written by the prophets, that should come.

"And when they had all gone forth and had witnessed for themselves, they did cry out with one accord, saying:

"Hosanna! Blessed be the name of the Most High God! And they did fall down at the feet of Jesus and did worship him." (3 Nephi 3-17)

Indian Traditions Indicate Christ's Visit

Jesus Christ spent three glorious days with the peoples of America. He organized his church and taught them the same doctrine he had delivered to his disciples in Jerusalem. As he left them he promised to come again. This historic visitation is supported by the traditions of all the Indians of America who have the same story, that their fathers were visited a long time ago by a fair God who taught his Gospel and blessed them, promising to return again. *The conquest of Peru and Mexico by a handful of white men was possible because of this tradition of the promised return of the white God.*

A Latter-day Witness that Jesus Lives

And now another witness which the Church furnishes that Jesus Christ not only lives but that he is deeply interested in this generation as he was in them of old is the witness of Joseph Smith and Oliver Cowdery that on the third day of April, 1836, one hundred years ago, in the Kirtland Temple, built by divine command to provide a place for the Lord's appearance, the following event occurred:

"We saw the Lord standing upon the breastwork of the pulpit, before us; and under his feet was a paved work of pure gold, in color like amber.

"His eyes were as a flame of fire; the hair of his head was white like the pure snow; his countenance shone above the brightness of the sun; and his voice was as the sound of the rushing of great waters, even the voice of Jehovah, saying:

"I am the first and the last; I am he who liveth, I am he who was slain; I am your advocate with the Father. (D&C 110:2-4).

A Great and Marvelous Work

He further announced that the purpose of his visit and the sending of prophets of ancient times, who held keys of authority, was to inaugurate the dispensation of the fulness of times spoken of by the prophets, wherein all keys and authority of all former dispensations were to be reintroduced among men in the building and establishment of Christ's kingdom triumphant in the earth to which he would come to rule and reign as King of kings and Lord of lords for a thousand years, as the prophets had foretold. Jesus announced in this dispensation, therefore, that the hour had come when a great and marvelous work was about to commence among men, wherein everything would be shaken that could be shaken and only the truth would stand, and that the prophecies of old were about to be fulfilled, when the Spirit of God would be poured out upon all flesh and old men should dream dreams and young men should see visions (Joel 2:28), and that as a result of it men would see wonders in the heavens and upon the earth.

What has happened in this world since that visitation a hundred years ago is in part at least a realization of the promise, far greater human progress has been made in the development of science in the last hundred years than in all the preceding ages combined. Surely the Spirit of God has been poured out upon all flesh, and men have caught visions of the secrets of God and the materialization of these visions has produced wonders in the heavens and upon the earth. The Lord's hand is in all that is now going forward. The conflict between good and evil will be fierce but out of every struggle will come the victory of the right and of the truth. Every man-made institution that stands in the way of God's purposes will be shaken and fall to the earth, and his kingdom shall come and his will be done upon earth as it is in heaven.

(CR October 1936, pp. 99-102)

The Path of Life

John A. Widtsoe

Elder John A. Widtsoe was a prominent Church leader for many years and a prolific exponent of the gospel principles. He contributed greatly to the missionary effort of the Church. The following is excerpted from the Handbook of the Restoration, published in 1944.

The Spirit is Eternal

An eternal spirit equipped with an imperishable body is capable of fullest joy and development. The body laid in the grave would have to be obtained again. The Father had so promised. This, the Son, the Christ, undertook to secure for the children of earth. Adam transgressed a law, a necessary transgression, so that his deathless spirit might become associated with a mortal body. He thereby became subject to death. *Adam's posterity inherited mortality and inevitable death.* By Adam's act, death came into the world; by the act of another, the consequences of death could be set aside, and the bodies of men resurrected into everlasting life. One man may cut the wires yielding light to a city; another may reunite them, and again flood the city with light.

Jesus Died that All Might Live

Jesus gave his life, his earthly life, that all mankind might be resurrected, and eternally enjoy the association of body and spirit. This was the atonement of Jesus, the Christ. The mystery of the process may be beyond our understanding, but the certainty of the immeasurable service to man remains.

Jesus did more than atone for the transgression of Adam. He brought to earth the principles of truth for man's guidance into happiness on earth and in heaven. This system of truth, the gospel, was taught father Adam; it was restated at various times, as men fell away from the truth; when Jesus came upon earth, he taught it in its simplicity to the people of his day; and in these days, after a long period of spiritual darkness, he has restored it again. Through the ages, Jesus, by prophets and by the inspiration that comes to every righteous man, has sought to hold Adam's children in a path of conduct that will lead them back into God's presence, there forever to taste the joy of unending, continuing progress. He has lighted the path of life for every willing traveler.

God Desires His Children to Have Joy

Jesus, by his own example, showed us how to obtain enduring happiness, which is, and should be, the object of every person. God desires his children to have joy. The attainment of a fully satisfying life comes from compliance with definite conditions. The foremost of these is that the searcher for happiness must overcome every desire and act that may be in opposition to the gospel code; for the cause of human salvation he must be ready to sacrifice his every earthly desire, his possessions, his all, his life if needs be. *Only in the spirit of sacrifice can the gift of eternal joy,* beginning on earth and continuing through all time, *be obtained and made secure.* Jesus suffered the hardships of life, relinquished the gifts of earth, gave his life, that all men might be brought into eternal happiness. His sacrifice was more than that of a man. His pains of suffering were exquisitely keen, for his understanding and organization were those of a God. He suffered for all, and the sacrifices and sufferings of all the world were concentrated in his agony as he hung upon the cross. The lesson of sacrifice was the culminating gift of his life. By this vast sacrifice, terrible as it must have been, he won great joy for himself—the joy of having opened the door of salvation to his brothers and sisters. His love for us made possible his sacrifice.

He is Our Redeemer

Such, then, is Jesus of Nazareth, the Son of God, our elder Brother, who has watched over the generations of men from the beginning of earth; who has taught and taught again the gospel message to a world hard of hearing and weak of will; who suffered the pains of the world and died that men might again possess their bodies, purified, imperishable; who by his example showed us the beauty and necessity of love and sacrifice; who still guides and leads and assists us; and who on the last great day will be our interpreter, our defender, our advocate with God, and bring us into eternal life.

He is our Redeemer.

(Handbook of the Restoration, 1944, pp. 195-197)

A Sacrifice for This Earth

Parley P. Pratt

Elder Parley P. Pratt was one of the Church's earliest writers. One of his better known works, "A Voice of Warning," *was first published in 1837. The following is taken from a discourse delivered in the Old Tabernacle in Salt Lake City, April 7, 1856, shortly more than one year before he was assassinated in Arkansas, May 13, 1857.*

Christ Died for All the Earth

Christ offered himself a sacrifice for this earth, for men, for the animals, for fishes, and the creeping things. Christ died for the earth and for the elements; Christ died for all mankind upon its face. Christ died, his blood was spilt, the priesthood was given, and the labor will continue with the Priesthood from generation to generation, until the kingdom will finally be given to the Saints to possess for ever and ever.

The Sons of Perdition are Lost Forever

He died to accomplish the salvation of all except the sons of perdition, and they have had all these blessings applied to them, and have partaken of them, known them, and then turned enemies to them, and there is not anything greater that you can do for them, and they perish, for after the blood of Christ has been shed and they despised it, nothing more can be done for them than already has been, for they have rejected the means of salvation.

If salt won't save me, what else will? If salt loses its saltness, what will salt the earth? All this was undertaken, and it will be carried through until every son and daughter of Adam have an opportunity of participating in its benefits. *(JD 3:315-316)*

A Perfect Pattern of Obedience

Amasa Lyman

Elder Amasa Lyman was a prominent figure in the Church and became a member of the Quorum of Twelve Apostles in 1842. After the Prophet Joseph Smith's death in 1844, he spoke in support of Brigham Young and the succession of the Twelve as the leading quorum of the Church. The following is from a discourse he delivered in the 9th Ward Schoolhouse in Salt Lake City on Christmas Day, 1859.

Jesus Lived and Died for Us

We will suppose that Jesus had come into the world and died on Calvary as he did, but that he had not left the principles of life in the world. Suppose he had never called the humble fishermen and endowed them, how much wiser would the world have been? Who would have been delivered from sin? Who would have realized the blessings of the Gospel of salvation? But Jesus lived, and Jesus died. Then what is it that should make us rejoice? It is that Jesus, who was here, has returned to the heavens,—that his work is done. We should also be thankful for the truths that he taught, for the many good things that he said, for the Priesthood he left, through which the gospel is revealed, and a medium opened through which you and I could be brought to the knowledge of the truth, accomplish that which will produce a deliverance from sin.

Jesus Brought the Priesthood to Man

Then let us not rejoice altogether because Jesus lived, or that he died in the world, but that coming into the world he brought with him the Priesthood—that he brought with him the power, the right to officiate as well as to teach the Gospel of life; and by virtue of his appointment he had power to appoint others to act in his name. When he was crucified, and for a few days left this state of existence, it was to open the door of salvation to a fallen world. Well, then, it is the Gospel, after all, for which we respect Jesus. There was nothing about Jesus but the Priesthood that he held and the Gospel that he proclaimed that was so very singular. But he died for the world. Yes; and what man that ever died for the truth that he died for, did not die for the world? Prophets have died in our day. Men have testified to the truth, and for that truth have died; but has their blood redeemed us from the sin and transgression we were previously guilty of? Have we found redemption through them? As far as we have obtained it, it has been by walking in the truth.

A Perfect Pattern of Obedience

Jesus, who was the bright and full reflection of the character of his Father, was himself a perfect pattern of obedience. *He not only recommended to the world obedience, but was himself a living pattern and example of that obedience which he taught,* and through that obedience merited that which was conferred upon him. Hence we read that he was exalted above his brethren, simply because he loved righteousness and hated iniquity; and it is that same principle that saves you and me. We may talk of men being redeemed by the efficacy of his blood; but the truth is that that blood has no efficacy to wash away our sins. That must depend upon our own action.

Can Jesus free us from sin while we go and sin again? What is it that frees us from sin? Did not Jesus preach the word of life? Yes. But who is it that shall believe—that shall be benefited and instructed? It is we that are to be redeemed. *(JD 7:298-299)*

The End of All Evil

Brigham Young

These remarks were delivered by President Young to the Saints assembled in the Bowery in Salt Lake City, July 8, 1860.

The Savior's Work not Finished

The Savior has not finished his work, and cannot receive the fulness of his glory until the influence and power of the wicked are overcome and brought into subjection. When the wicked inhabitants of the earth, the beasts of the field, fowls of the air, fish of the sea, all mineral substances, and all else pertaining to this earth, are overcome, then he will take the kingdom, present it to the Father, and say, "Here is the work you gave me to do—you made the appointment—I have wrought faithfully, and here are my brethren and sisters who have wrought with me. We have wrought faithfully together; we have overcome the flesh, hell, and the Devil. I have overcome, they have followed in my footsteps, and here are all thou hast given me; I have lost none, except the son of perdition."

Jesus suffered himself to be crowned with thorns and crucified; but suppose he had said, "I will not make this great sacrifice; I am the Almighty; I will dash my enemies to pieces, and I will not die for the world," what would have been the result? Jesus would have become a son of perdition; he would have lost every power and right to the kingdom he was about to redeem—would have become no better than the son of the morning who contended against him, and would have contended against righteousness from that time, and against whoever the Lord would then appoint to destroy sin and death, and him that had the power of it.

Cling to Light Rather than Darkness

We can follow darkness and death, if we choose; but let us cling to light instead of darkness, malice, hatred, wrath, and bitterness; for Jesus will make an end of all evil. Himself is all that man has to give for wisdom. *(JD 8:118)*

Christ Preached to the Spirits in Prison

John Taylor

President Taylor was in the Ogden Tabernacle on Sunday, March 21, 1880, when he made these remarks to the members of the Church.

The Savior had a Special Mission

After some thousands of years (after the flood) Jesus came, associated with another dispensation. And when he appeared on the earth and had got through with his ministry, and had suffered in the flesh and was quickened by the spirit, "he went and preached to the spirits in prison" who were, as stated, "sometime disobedient in the days of Noah." And hence thousands of people that had suffered the wrath of God for so long a time had the opportunity of listening to the principles of the Gospel in another dispensation that Jesus came to proclaim. And when he had got through with his mission on the earth to those who lived, he went then to preach to those who had been dead, and I might properly say were damned for so many years. And what was the special mission he had to proclaim? He came "to preach the Gospel to the poor, to open the eyes of the blind, to set at liberty those that were bound, and to preach the acceptable year of the Lord, and the day of vengeance of our God." That was part of his mission; *the whole of his mission, however, has not yet been fulfilled.* But he came to liberate the prisoners, which he did in the spirit, when he got through with his mission on the earth. *(JD 21:243-244)*

Jesus Christ is the Son of God

Joseph Fielding Smith

President Joseph Fielding Smith's understanding of the scriptures and the doctrines of the Church far surpassed most of the members of the Church in his time. In 1910, when he was 33 years old, he was ordained an apostle and set apart as a member of the Quorum of the Twelve. In 1970, he became the tenth President of the Church.

Jesus Christ is the Son of God

If there is any one thing that brings joy and peace and satisfaction to the heart of man, beyond anything else that I know of, it is the abiding testimony which I have, and which you have, that Jesus Christ is the Son of God. That is a truth that cannot be changed. Men may attack it; they may ridicule it; they may declare that he is not the Redeemer of the world, that his mission was not true, or that its purpose, through the shedding of his blood, was not to grant unto all men the remission of sins on condition of their repentance. They may refuse to believe in the resurrection from the dead, or even that Christ himself came forth, as the Scriptures declare, after he had been put to death by his enemies; nevertheless the truth remains. *He did die for the sins of the world, he did bring to pass redemption from death, he did grant unto men the opportunity of repentance,* and remission of sins through their belief and acceptance of the principles of the gospel, and of his mission. These truths are fundamental, they shall endure; they cannot be destroyed no matter what men may say or think. Furthermore, the mission of Jesus Christ teaches us that there was a time when men departed from the truth, when transgression came into the world, and man, through his agency sinned, or violated a law, which brought death upon the world. For Christ came to atone for sin, to bring again the restitution of life, of peace, of happiness, through the things which he suffered. Now anything which is contrary to that is not true.

All Must Accept the Atonement

I bear witness . . . that there is no place in The Church of Jesus Christ of Latter-day Saints for the man who does not accept without reservation, the atonement of the Lord Jesus Christ, who does not believe that his mission in this world was to redeem, to restore, to grant again unto man the privilege, through his faith, through his repentance, and his worthiness, the opportunity of coming back again into the presence of God the Father and his Son, Jesus Christ. If there are within the Church those who have these so-called modernist tendencies, who deny the miracles of Christ, the miracles of the scriptures, the doctrines known as the gospel of Jesus Christ, who cannot accept him as the Redeemer of the world, then they should repent of their sins, for it is within the power, and it is *the privilege of each individual member of this Church to know the truth for himself,* through the gift and the power of the Holy Ghost. There need be no doubt, no uncertainty, in regard to this matter. The Lord has taught us these principles in modern revelation. He declared them while in his ministry upon the earth.

(CR October 1924, pp. 100-101)

The Noblest of All the Sons of God

George F. Richards

Elder Richards became a member of the Quorum of Twelve Apostles in 1906. In 1945, he became the President of that Quorum. He made these remarks in April General Conference, at Salt Lake City, in 1912.

Christ Did All that was Required of Him

In the hearts of the Latter-day Saints there are two names very closely associated, and very dear to us—the name of our beloved Savior, Jesus Christ, and our dear Prophet, Joseph Smith. The mission and labors of these two were not entirely unlike. We look upon the former as the noblest of all the sons of God, as the first born of our Eternal Father in the spirit, and the only begotten of the Father in the flesh, the Creator of all things, under the direction of the Father, the Redeemer and Savior of the world who *voluntarily* gave Himself to a life of sorrow and affliction, of trial and temptation, on whom was heaped all manner of indignities, who resisted all temptations to do evil, who denied Himself everything that was forbidden in the law of the Gospel, of which He was the author. He did all things that were required of Him, doing the will of the Father under all circumstances, and finally gave His life, a martyr, sacrifice upon the cross of Calvary, for all of our Father's children.

That We Might Be Redeemed

This He did that we might be redeemed from the original sin, that we might live again as immortal beings; that after we have laid off these mortal bodies, our spirits shall take upon themselves again bodies which shall not be subject to death, nor to suffering as here in the flesh; also that we might be redeemed from the effects of our own sins and transgressions, and be saved with Him in our Father's kingdom, through obedience on our part to the laws and ordinances of the Gospel. We do love the Lord, Jesus Christ, our Savior. *(CR April 1912, pp. 37-38)*

All Mankind Redeemed

Orson F. Whitney

Elder Orson F. Whitney spoke in April Conference, 1927, in Salt Lake City. The following is taken from his longer discourse.

The Savior's Mission is Universal

Christ redeemed all mankind, "treading the wine press alone," but the House of Israel prepared the way for his coming, and continued the work that he began. This is especially true of the prophets who foretold his advent, and the apostles who preached his gospel to Jew and gentile. Nor let the modern apostles, seventies and elders be overlooked, who are now preaching the gospel to the Gentiles, and ere long will carry it to the Jews.

Nobody, I hope, connects the Savior's mighty mission only with the age in which he was crucified. That was but a part of it. The death on Calvary was no more the ending of that divine career, than the birth at Bethlehem was its beginning. *The Savior's mission is universal, extending from eternity into time and back again into eternity.* All the ages of the past, all the gospel dispensations, from Adam to Joseph Smith, are parts of the all-embracing mission of the world's Redeemer. It is all Christ's work, from the hour of his election in the Eternal Councils, down to the Millennial Reign, during which he will sanctify the earth and prepare it for celestial glory. *(CR April 1927, p. 101)*

A Fundamental Principle

". . . I am the resurrection and the life: he that believeth in me, though he were dead, yet shall he live." (John 11:25)

A Basic Tenet of the Gospel

Hugh B. Brown

Elder Brown served more than 20 years as a General Authority of the Church. He began in 1953 with a call as an Assistant to the Twelve. Five years later he was ordained an Apostle. In 1961, he was called into the First Presidency and served as a member of that quorum until President McKay's death in 1970. Elder Brown passed away in December, 1975. The following is from his remarks to April General Conference, 1962.

All Mankind May Be Saved Through the Atonement

. . . There is one doctrinal event (of the Gospel of Christ), which foreshadows and overshadows all other Christian doctrine. I refer to the atonement of Christ, and it would seem that this would be appropriate, as we approach the Easter time. "We believe that through the atonement of Christ, all mankind may be saved, by obedience to the laws and ordinances of the Gospel." (Third Article of Faith)

Faith in this one transcendent event, the most important in all history, *is the enduring foundation upon which the true Christian gospel is built.* Upon it, the salvation of the whole human family depends. He who understands and accepts the full significance of the vicarious sacrifice of Jesus Christ and conforms to the principles and ordinances which that acceptance enjoins may be properly classified as a Christian.

Faith Alone Is Not Sufficient

But there must be more than mere lip service; faith alone is not sufficient.

Jesus said: "Wherefore by their fruits ye shall know them.

"Not every one that saith unto me, Lord, Lord, shall enter into the kingdom of heaven; but he that doeth the will of my Father which is in heaven." (Matthew 7:20 21)

What must one do to become a Christian or to be saved is an ancient and oft-repeated question which was answered by Peter, the apostle, on the day of Pentecost, when through his powerful sermon the people were convinced and pricked in their hearts and cried out: "Men and brethren, what shall we do?" and the apostle said, ". . . Repent, and be baptized every one of you in the name of Jesus Christ for the remission of sins, and ye shall receive the gift of the Holy Ghost." (Acts 2:38)

Forgiveness is a Basic Principle of the Gospel

Forgiveness on terms of repentance is a basic Christian principle. But is one saved by merely meeting these preliminary requirements? The Apostle Paul, in one of his dynamic letters, said, speaking of these principles: ". . . let us go on unto perfection; not laying again the foundation of repentance from dead works, and of faith toward God." (Hebrews 6:1)

And he adds that the work of perfecting the Saints (the people of the Church in former days were known as Saints) must continue "Till we all come in the unity of the faith, and of the knowledge of the Son of God, unto a perfect man, unto the measure of the stature of the fulness of Christ." (Ephesians 4:13)

Salvation is Like Education

Salvation is a continuing, on-going process. It is eternally improving, achieving, becoming—yes, and overcoming. In some ways it may be analogous to education, which is a continuous process of overcoming ignorance. When is a man educated? When is a man saved? *We believe a man is saved no faster than he gains knowledge for "the glory of God is intelligence."* (See D&C 93:36)

Is a man educated when he enrolls in college, or when he gets his bachelor's, his master's or doctorate? Yes, relatively he is an educated man, but he still has a lifetime—an eternity, in fact, in which to pursue knowledge and truth. The highest reaches of life are but embryonic in the light of eternity, and man has every reason to hope that a future life will afford him full scope for larger and fuller achievement.

Active Acceptance of All Gospel Principles is Required

This Church, which bears Christ's name, has from the beginning uniformly taught that faith in the Lord Jesus Christ is the first saving principle of the gospel, but as the poet tells us, "Heaven is not gained by a single bound, but we build the ladders by which we rise, from the lowly earth to the vaulted skies, and mount to its summit round by round."

Faith must be confirmed and demonstrated by active acceptance of all the other principles and ordinances taught by him whose name is incorporated in the word Christian.

We do not claim to understand fully the atonement in all of its limitless scope and infinite blessing; but God has revealed enough detail concerning the need, purpose, and universal application of the atonement of Christ to justify the doctrine that the resurrection from the dead is assured to all men.

John said: "and I saw the dead, small and great, stand before God; and the books were opened: and another book was opened, which is the book of life: and the dead were judged out of those things which were written in the books, according to their works." (Rev. 20:12)

Exaltation May Be Progressively Attained

Eternal life and exaltation, however, made possible by the vicarious sacrifice of Christ may be progressively attained by man's voluntary cooperation with divine will and purpose. When we think of any reconciliation or appeasement or settlement, we consider it in connection with some previous act or event of which it is a sequel. For instance, a treaty of peace is a sequel of war. A settlement of a claim or an obligation implies there has been an account with a debit balance. When we speak of the atonement wrought by Jesus Christ, we envision an unpaid debt, and antecedent transgression; something to atone for.

All students of the Bible who accept the New Testament see in his atonement a sequel to the transgression of Adam, generally known as the Fall of Adam. Through the Fall, Adam and Eve and all their posterity became subject to bodily disintegration and death and also to banishment from the presence of God, which is in the nature of spiritual death, and this despite the fact that the cause was individual transgression. By the individual atonement of Christ, free redemption from the transgression of Adam is assured to all. Paul assures us that: ". . . since by man came death, by man came also the resurrection of the dead.

"For as in Adam all die, even so in Christ shall all be made alive." (I Corinthians 15:21-22)

Adam's Transgression was Foreseen

The transgression of Adam, together with all of its consequences, was foreseen and the expiation provided for before the foundations of the world were laid. In that primeval council, of which the scriptures speak, when "all the sons of God shouted for joy" (see Job 38:7), Christ offered himself as a ransom. He was not coerced or required to make this sacrifice. His free agency was in no way infringed or trammeled. It was a freewill, love-inspired offer, which could have been withdrawn at any time. It was optional until the very time of his crucifixion. He gently rebuked Peter, you remember, who would have defended him with a sword at the time of the betrayal, and Jesus said: "Thinkest thou that I cannot now pray to my Father, and he shall presently give me more than twelve legions of angels?" (Matthew 26:53)

The question is sometimes asked: Why was such a sacrifice of God's beloved Son permitted or accepted? Why not let someone else pay that debt? Why not Adam?

Only Christ was Sinless

The answer is found in the fact that of all the sons of God, only Christ could qualify, because he was the only sinless man who ever walked the earth. Furthermore, he was the First Begotten, the eldest of the sons of God in the spirit, and the Only Begotten in the flesh, and therefore the only one who possessed the full powers of Godhood and manhood. Hear him refer to that premortal existence in the most beautiful prayer on record, found in the 17th chapter of John; he prayed: "And now, O Father, glorify thou me with thine own self with the glory which I had with thee before the world was." (John 17:5)

Christ was the only one wholly free from the dominion of Satan, the only one possessed of power to hold death in abeyance and to die only as he willed so to do, the only one who could conquer death. He said: "for as the Father hath life in himself; so hath he given to the Son to have life in himself." (John 5:26)

And again: "Therefore doth my Father love me, because I lay down my life, that I might take it again.

"No man taketh it from me, but I lay it down of myself. I have power to lay it down, and I have power to take it again . . ." (John 10:17-18)

Obedience and Love Motivated the Savior's Sacrifice

Another question is sometimes heard: Why should Christ have volunteered to make this sacrifice? What was the motive that inspired and sustained him from the time of that council in heaven until the moment of his agonized cry, "It is finished"? (John 19:30)

The answer to this question is two-fold: first, his undeviating devotion to his Father's will. He said: ". . . My meat is to do the will of him that sent me, and to finish his work." (Ibid. 4:34)

Second was his supernatural and all-embracing love for mankind, who, without his mediation, would have remained in the total gloom of desiring without hope throughout eternity.

As the late President Taylor very beautifully and very truthfully said, speaking of the atonement: "Is justice dishonored? No; it is satisfied, the debt is paid. Is righteousness departed from? No; this is a righteous act. All requirements are met. Is judgment violated? No; its demands are fulfilled. Is mercy triumphant? No; she simply claims her own. Justice, judgment, mercy and truth all harmonize as the attributes of Deity. 'Justice and truth have met together, righteousness and peace have kissed each other.' Justice and judgment triumph as well as mercy and peace." (The Mediation and Atonement, 1950 edition, p. 167)

There Could Be No Alternative to the Atonement

What was the alternative to the atonement? What if there had been no atonement? If there had been no atonement, all men would have been doomed to eternal death, for unless Christ had broken its bonds, death would have been victorious. All who died before the Meridian of Time were still in their graves when Christ came forth triumphantly from the tomb and broke the bonds that held them captive.

Matthew records that: " . . . the graves were opened; and many bodies of the Saints which slept arose,

"And came out of the graves after his resurrection, and went into the holy city, and appeared unto many." (Matthew 27:52-53)

Thus he became the first fruits of them that slept. When the Apostle Paul comprehended the full meaning of this unprecedented event, he joyfully exclaimed: "O death, where is thy sting? O grave, where is thy victory? (I Corinthians 15:55)

And Jesus comforted and reassured all the grieving Marthas of the world with these immortal words: ". . . *I am the resurrection, and the life: he that believeth in me, though he were dead, yet shall he live:*

"And whosoever liveth and believeth in me shall never die . . ." (John 11:25-26)

Forgiveness May Be Obtained for Sins

But the victory over death is not the only benefit arising from the atonement of the Messiah; his atonement not only liberated all men from eternal death but, through the atonement, forgiveness of our individual sins may be obtained. He made it possible for us, through faith, repentance, and continued righteousness, to obtain absolution from the effects of personal sins. One does not get the full benefit of the atonement simply by acknowledging it.

Men cannot be saved in their sins because, by divine decree, no unclean thing can enter the kingdom of heaven; however, *through repentance, baptism and the power of the Holy Ghost, men may be saved from their sins.*

No man can by one single act, however great or sincere, free himself from the necessity for that "patient continuance in well doing" of which Paul speaks. He must still follow the Master and endure to the end. Jesus plainly and impressively taught this truth to the young man who came to him saying:

". . . Good Master, what good thing shall I do, that I may have eternal life?

"And he said unto him, Why callest thou me good? There is none good but one, that is, God: but if thou wilt enter into life, keep the commandments.

"He saith unto him, which? Jesus said, Thou shalt do no murder, Thou shalt not commit adultery, Thou shalt not steal, Thou shalt not bear false witness,

"Honor thy father and thy mother: and, Thou shalt love thy neighbor as thyself.

"The young man saith unto him, All these things have I kept from my youth up; what lack I yet?

"Jesus said unto him, If thou wilt be perfect, go and sell that thou hast, and give to the poor, and thou shalt have treasure in heaven: and come and follow me." (Matthew 19:16-21)

We Must Follow the Master

It is not enough therefore merely to keep the commandments or obey the law nor even to sell all and give to the poor. The final requirement is to follow the Master. The poet has us sing:

"Jesus, I my cross have taken, all to leave and follow thee;

"Naked, poor, despised, forsaken, thou from hence my all shall be.

"Perish every fond ambition, all I've thought, or hoped, or known;

"Yet how rich is my condition, God and Heaven are still my own!"

That all men are sinners in varying degrees is repeatedly affirmed in the New Testament. Paul wrote to the Romans: "For all have sinned, and come short of the glory of God." (Romans 3:23)

And John adds: "If we say that we have no sin, we deceive ourselves, and the truth is not in us." (I John 1:8)

Peter said: "And beside this, giving all diligence, add to your faith virtue; and to virtue knowledge;

"And to knowledge temperance; and to temperance patience; and to patience godliness;

"And to godliness brotherly kindness; and to brotherly kindness charity.

"For if these things be in you, and abound, they make you that ye shall neither be barren nor unfruitful in the knowledge of our Lord Jesus Christ." (II Peter 1:5-8)

That the blessings of the atonement are to be made available not only to all who lived before the time of Christ, but also to all who die without an opportunity to hear the gospel is evidenced by Peter's declaration: "For for this cause was the gospel preached also to them that are dead, that they might be judged according to men in the flesh, but live according to God in the spirit." (I Peter 4:6)

The Savior himself confirms this as follows: "Verily, verily, I say unto you, The hour is coming, and now is, when the dead shall hear the voice of the Son of God: and they that hear shall live." (John 5:25) *(CR April 1962, pp. 106-110)*

The Atoning Sacrifice Foreshadowed

B. H. Roberts

The Church's most prominent historian, Elder Roberts, became a member of the First Council of Seventy in October, 1888. His contributions include editing the seven volume "Documentary History of the Church," writing the six-volume "Comprehensive History of the Church," and several books on the history and doctrines of Mormonism. For five years he prepared study courses for the Seventies quorums. The following selection is from The Seventy's Course in Theology.

Old Testament Sacrifices Were of Divine Origin

From the earliest times the fact of an Atonement for man is foreshadowed. "The serpent beguiled me, and I did eat," said Eve, to the Lord. "And the Lord God said unto the serpent, . . . I will put enmity between thee and the woman, and between thy seed and her seed; it shall bruise thy head, and thou shalt bruise his heel." (Gen. 3:13, 15)

In this passage Christians with justice have always seen the proclamation of the good tidings of the final victory over sin. "It is in Christ that the seed of the woman crushes the serpent."

The Atonement is also foreshadowed in the sacrifices of burnt offerings of Adam, his son Abel and the early Bible patriarchs. So meager is the Bible account of the origin of sacrifices that some have doubted if they bore any relation to the sacrifice to be offered by the Christ, or were at all of divine origin. Our scripture, however, the Book of Moses, sets the matter at rest for Latter-day Saints; for there it is written:

"And Adam and Eve, his wife, called upon the name of the Lord, and they heard the voice of the Lord from the way toward the Garden of Eden, speaking unto them, and they saw him not; for they were shut out from his presence. And he gave unto them commandments, that they should worship the Lord their God, and should offer the firstlings of their flocks, for an offering unto the Lord. And Adam was obedient unto the commandments of the Lord. And after many days an angel of the Lord appeared unto Adam, saying: Why dost thou offer sacrifices unto the Lord? And Adam said unto him, I know not, save the Lord commanded me. And then the angel spake saying: This thing is a similitude of the sacrifice of the Only Begotten of the Father, which is full of grace and truth. Wherefore, thou shalt do all that thou doest in the name of the Son, and thou shalt repent and call upon God in the name of the Son forevermore. And in that day the Holy Ghost fell upon Adam, which beareth record of the Father and the Son, saying: I am the only begotten of the Father from the beginning, henceforth and forever, that as thou hast fallen thou mayest be redeemed, and all mankind, even as many as will."

This clearly establishes the divine origin of sacrifices among the antediluvian patriarchs; and, indeed, of all antiquity; and also the fact, that they but foreshadowed the great sacrifice to be made in due time by the Son of God himself. Doctor Wm. Smith, the author of the "Old Testament History," says:

"The curse upon the serpent and promise to the woman point clearly to a Redeemer, who should be born of a woman, and by his own suffering, should destroy the power of the devil; and here we have the first prophecy of the Messiah. . . . *There can be no reasonable doubt that the sacrifice of living animals was now instituted as a prophetic figure of the great sacrifice which should fulfill this promise.* Animals must have been slain to provide the skins that clothed Adam and Eve; and wherefore slain, except in sacrifice? This might not seem conclusive in itself; but the whole reason for sacrifice began to exist now; its use is taken for granted in the next chapter (Gen. 4); and it continues throughout the patriarchal age without the record of any other beginning.

Without the Shedding of Blood Sin Cannot Be Remitted

"Thus early, then, man learned that, 'without shedding of blood, there is no remission of sin;' that his own forfeited life was redeemed, and to be restored by the sacrifice of the coming 'seed of the woman;' and that he was placed by God under a new dispensation of mercy. Nay, even his punishment was a mercy; for his suffering was a discipline to train him in submission to God's will. The repentance of our first parents is nowhere expressly stated; but it is implied here and in the subsequent narrative."

The fact of Adam's repentance, however, is clearly set forth in the Book of Moses, and his acceptance of the whole scheme of salvation through the atonement of Christ.

It is very generally conceded that the sacrifices and obligations of the Mosaic ritual have a direct relationship to the great atoning sacrifice to be made by the Christ. From the ninth and tenth chapters of the Epistle to the Hebrews it is evident that "the law" was "a shadow of good things to come;" the law's sacrifices for sin and reconciliation with God but figured forth the greater and more efficient sacrifice to be made by the Son of God; nay, whatever of virtue there was in the sacrifices of the law were dependent upon the great sacrifice to follow.

Animal Sacrifices Were Only Symbols

Of themselves, the sacrifices of the law had no virtue at all unconnected with the sacrifice to be made by the Christ; they were but symbols figuring forth that sacrifice in which the virtue was, the sacrifice of the Christ himself. "For it is expedient," says the Nephite Prophet Alma—"It is expedient that an Atonement should be made; for according to the great plan of the eternal God, there must be an Atonement made, or else all mankind must unavoidably perish; yea, all are hardened; yea, all are fallen and are lost, and must perish except it be through the Atonement which it is expedient should be made. Therefore, *it is expedient that there should be a great and last sacrifice; and then shall there be, or it is expedient there should be, a stop to the shedding of blood; then shall the law of Moses be fulfilled;* yea, it shall be all fulfilled; every jot and tittle, and none shall have passed away. And behold, this is the whole meaning of the law; every whit pointing to that great and last sacrifice; and that great and last sacrifice will be the Son of God; yea, infinite and eternal." (Alma 34:9, 13, 14)

The late President John Taylor upon this subject said:

"These sacrifices, which were offered up from the days of Adam until the time of our Savior's advent, were typical of the great expiatory sacrifice which He was to make by the sacrifice of himself. They were so many types, shadows and forms of which he was the great prototype—the substance, the reality prefigured and foreshadowed by the other sacrifices which had been offered up from the beginning.

"When the law was given to Moses, all the forms pertaining to the sacrificial ceremonies were revealed in detail, and the instructions in relation thereto were not simply of a general nature, but they entered into minute particulars in relation to all things connected with those who officiated, the form and pattern of the sacred utensils and of the vestments of the priesthood, the creatures to be sacrificed, the order of the proceedings, and indeed of all matters associated with the observance of these rites. Almost the whole of the book of Leviticus, and considerable of the book of Numbers, is occupied with these instructions and kindred matters. This Mosaic law, with all its duties, observances, ceremonies and sacrifices, continued in force until Christ's death."

The Nature of Animal Sacrifices

The author of the article on "Sacrifices," in Smith's "Bible Dictionary" (Hackett edition), Vol. IV—Rev. Alfred Barry, Fellow of Trinity College, Cambridge, in describing the "Sin Offering of the Mosaic Law," says:

"The nature and meaning of the various kinds of sacrifice is partly gathered from the form of their institution and ceremonial, partly from the teaching of the prophets, and partly from the New Testament, especially the Epistle to the Hebrews. All had relation, under different aspects, to a covenant between God and man.

"The sin offering represented that covenant as broken by man, and as knit together again, by God's appointment, through the 'shedding of blood.' Its characteristic ceremony was the sprinkling of the blood before the veil of the sanctuary, the putting some of it on the horns of the altar, incense, and the pouring out of all the rest at the foot of the altar of burnt offering. The flesh was in no case touched by the offerer; either it was consumed by fire without the camp, or it was eaten by the priest alone in the holy place, and everything that touched it was holy. This latter point marked the distinction from the peace-offering, and showed that the sacrificer had been rendered unworthy of communion with God. The shedding of blood, the symbol of life, signified that the death of the offender was deserved for sin, but that the death of the victim was accepted for his death by the ordinance of God's mercy."

"This (the truth of the preceding paragraph) is seen most clearly in the ceremonial of the 'Day of Atonement,' when, after the sacrifice of the one goat, the high priest's hand was laid on the head of the scape-goat—which was the other part of the sin-offering—with confession of the sins of the people, that it might visibly bear them away, and so bring out explicitly, what in other sin-offerings was but implied. Accordingly we find that, in all cases, it was the custom for the offerer to lay his hand on the head of the sin-offering, to confess generally or specially his sins, and to say, 'Let this be my expiation.' Beyond all doubt, the sin-offering distinctly witnessed that sin existed in man, that the 'wages of that sin was death,' and that God had provided an Atonement by the vicarious suffering of an appointed victim. The reference of the Baptist to a 'Lamb of God who taketh away the sins of the world,' was one understood and hailed at once by a 'true Israelite.' "

The Establishment of the Passover

In some respects the Paschal Sacrifice more perfectly than any other, perhaps, foreshadowed the future sacrifice of the Son of God for the deliverance of his people—those who would trust the sign of deliverance in his blood. The institution of the sacrifice and feast was as follows. When all other judgements upon Pharoah failed to persuade him to let God's people go, then said the Lord to Moses:

"About midnight will I go out into the midst of Egypt: and all the first-born in the land of Egypt shall die, from the first-born of Pharoah that sitteth upon his throne, even unto the first-born of the maid-servant that is behind the mill; and all the first-born of beasts. And there shall be a great cry throughout all the land of Egypt, such as there was none like it, nor shall be like it any more. But against any of the children of Israel shall not a dog move his tongue, against man or beast; that ye may know how that the Lord doth put a difference between the Egyptians and Israel." (Exodus 9:4-7)

When this terrible judgment was about to be executed the Lord provided the following means of deliverance for his people: Each family in Israel were commanded at a given time to take a lamb without blemish, a male of the first year, for a Passover Offering, and it was to be killed in the evening.

"And they shall take of the blood and strike it on the two sideposts, and on the upper doorpost of the houses, wherein they shall eat it. And they shall eat the flesh in that night, roast with fire, and unleavened bread; and with bitter herbs they shall eat it. . . . And ye shall eat it in haste; it is the Lord's passover. For I will pass through the land of Egypt this night, and will smite all the first-born in the land of Egypt, both man and beast: and against all the gods of Egypt, I will execute judgment: I am the Lord. And the blood shall be to you for a token upon the houses where ye are: and when I see the blood, I will pass over you, and the plague shall not be upon you to destroy you, when I smite the land of Egypt. And this day shall be unto you for a memorial; and ye shall keep it a feast to the Lord throughout your generations: ye shall keep it a feast by an ordinance forever." (Exodus 12)

Thus was the Passover established. Of it the late President Taylor said:

"It appears, that when the destroying angel passed by the houses of the children of Israel he found the blood of a lamb sprinkled on the doorpost; which was a type of the blood of Christ, the lamb of God. The angel who was the executor of justice could not touch those who were protected by that sacred symbol; because that pre-figured the sacrifice of the Son of God, which was provided at the beginning of creation for the redemption of the human family, and which was strictly in accordance with provisions then made by the Almighty for that purpose—'the Lamb slain from before the foundation of the world'—and accepted in full as an atonement for the transgressions of mankind, according to the requirements of eternal justice and agreed to by the Savior and his Father."

Of course it cannot be doubted that this festival of the Passover was instituted as a great memorial of the deliverance from Egyptian bondage, and the birth of the nation of Israel; and there are not wanting those who maintain that this was its primary significance. But the leading feature in the festival, the Paschal Lamb, "a male, without blemish," the killing of it; the blood sprinkled on the door post, the sign of safety to God's people; the eating of the lamb in preparation of the journey; the subsequent honoring of this feast by the Christ with his disciples; the substitution of the Sacrament of the Lord's Supper for the Passover festival at the very time and on the very occasion of celebrating the feast of the Passover among the Jews; together with the subsequent inspired reference to Christ as the Paschal Lamb of the Christians, are circumstances too numerous and too nearly related to doubt of the significance of the Passover festival having reference to the great sacrifice to be made by the Son of God through the shedding of his blood in atonement for the deliverance of his people. Of the Passover being a symbol of the sacrifice of the Son of God, the writer upon that theme in Smith's "Bible Dictionary," says:

"No other 'shadow of good things to come' contained in the law can vie with the festival of the passover in expressiveness and completeness. Hence we are so often reminded of it, more or less distinctly, in the ritual and language of the church. Its outline, considered in reference to the great deliverance of the Israelites which it commemorated, and many of its minute details, have been appropriated as current expressions of the truths which God has revealed to us in the fullness of times in sending his Son upon earth."
(The Seventy's Course in Theology, Fourth Year (1911), pp. 46-53)

An Eternal Principle

Brigham Young

President Young delivered his remarks in this selection at the Tabernacle, Ogden, Utah on July 10, 1870.

We Have Contracted a Divine Debt

A divine debt has been contracted by the children, and the Father demands recompense. He says to his children on this earth, who are in sin and transgression, it is impossible for you to pay this debt; I have prepared a sacrifice; I will send my Only Begotten Son to pay this divine debt. Was it necessary then that Jesus should die? Do we understand why he should sacrifice his life? The idea that the Son of God, who never committed sin, should sacrifice his life, is unquestionably preposterous to the minds of many in the Christian world. But the fact exists that the Father, *the Divine Father,* whom we serve, the God of the universe, the God and Father of our Lord Jesus Christ, and the Father of our spirits, *provided this sacrifice and sent his son to die for us;* and it is also a great fact that the Son came to do the will of the Father, and that he has paid the debt, in fulfillment of the scripture which says, "He was the Lamb slain from the foundation of the world."

The Plan is the Same on All of God's Creations

Is it so on any other earth? On every earth. How many earths are there? I observed this morning that you may take the particles of matter composing this earth, and if they could be enumerated they would only be a beginning to the number of the creations of God; and they are continually coming into existence, and undergoing changes and passing through the same experience that we are passing through. *Sin is upon every earth that ever was created,* and if it was not so, I would like some philosophers to let us know how people can be exalted to become sons of God, and enjoy a fulness of glory with the Redeemer. Consequently *every earth has its redeemer,* and *every earth has its tempter;* and every earth, and the people thereof, in their turn and time, receive all that we receive, and pass through all the ordeals that we are passing through.

Only a Savior Can Pay the Eternal Debt

Is this easy to understand? It is perfectly easy to me; and my advice to those who have queries and doubts on this subject is, when they reason and philosophize upon it, not to plant their position in falsehood or argue hypothetically, but upon the facts as they exist, and they will come to the conclusion that unless God provides a Savior to pay this debt it can never be paid. Can all the wisdom of the world devise means by which we can be redeemed, and return to the presence of our Father and elder brother, and dwell with holy angels and celestial beings? No; it is beyond the power and wisdom of the inhabitants of the earth that now live, or that ever did or ever will live, to prepare or create a sacrifice that will pay this divine debt. But God provided it, and his Son has paid it, and we, each and every one, can now receive the truth and be saved in the kingdom of God. Is it clear and plain? It is to me, and if you have the Spirit of God, it is as plain to you as anything else in the world. *(JD 14:71-72)*

Importance of the Atonement

Orson Pratt

This selection has been taken from Elder Pratt's remarks in the 13th Ward assembly rooms, Salt Lake City, December 29, 1872.

One of the Most Important Events

We are, this afternoon, commemorating according to our usual custom, one of the most important events that has ever transpired in our world, and one which most concerns the whole human family, namely, the death and sufferings of the Lord Jesus Christ for the redemption of the human family. No other event can be compared with this in its importance, and in its bearings upon the human family. Everything else is but of a secondary consideration, when compared with the atonement that has been wrought out in behalf of man by the great Redeemer, yet, strange to say, there are those in the Christian world, so called, who profess to believe in Christianity and yet deny the efficacy of the atoning blood that was shed by our Lord and Savior Jesus Christ. More especially has this been the case for a few years past. I suppose there are many thousands who deny this now, where there were but few at the time of the rise of this Church. This has arisen, probably, from the multiplication of spiritual influences, which now prevail to a very great extent in the Chrisitan world--influences that are evil, revelations, false visions, spirit rappings and mediums. Almost without exception these false spirits have taught those who have listened to them, that there is no efficacy in the Atonement.

The Atonement is at the Foundation of the World

There is no subject more fully developed and made manifest to the children of men in modern revelation than that of the atonement. Much is said in relation to other doctrines, all of which have a bearing on the atonement, that lying at the foundation of the whole. If the evil one can prevail over the human family so as to get them to deny this fundamental doctrine, he knows that they are safe, so far as serving him and failing of their salvation are concerned. If they can only be wrought upon and deluded so as to disbelieve in the doctrine of the atonement, it does not matter to Satan what else they may believe. It is not my intention, however, this afternoon, unless so led by the Spirit of the Lord, to dwell much on this subject. It is one that has been so thoroughly taught to the Latter-day Saints, that I esteem it almost unnecessary to repeat that with which they are so familiar.

The Lord's Supper Commemorates the Atonement

By partaking of the Lord's Supper every Sabbath day, we commemorate that great event. If we do not preach so much about it by word of mouth we certainly fulfill the commandment which God has given requiring us to remember unto the Father the crucified body and shed blood of his Son, without which there would have been no remission of sin, and no redemption and mankind would have remained in their fallen state. No light could have penetrated the hearts of the children of men, and *there would have been no resurrection, no exaltation in the kingdom of God without the atonement.* When we speak of total depravity, it has reference to certain conditions. Man is not totally depraved now, and the reason is, there has been an atonement; but do away with that, as many do, and total depravity would reign, and men would live and die totally degraded beings. All the light that has come into the world, and that comes into the world, has come by reason of the atonement.

(JD 15:253-254)

Significance of the Atonement

Joseph Fielding Smith

Joseph Fielding Smith, while an Apostle, delivered this discourse to the members of the church assembled in the Tabernacle in Salt Lake City for April General Conference, 1956.

The Resurrection of Christ

At this season of the year the attention of Christians everywhere is centered on the resurrection of our Lord Jesus Christ. It is well that it is so; for *this is the most important event that ever occurred* in our fallen world. When Adam and Eve were placed in the Garden of Eden, there was no death. It was by the violation of a commandment that brought mortality and death upon them. The Lord said to them:

". . .Of every tree of the garden thou mayest freely eat: But of the tree of the knowledge of good and evil, thou shalt not eat of it: for in the day that thou eatest thereof thou shalt surely die." (Genesis 2:16, 17)

After they had eaten, the Lord cursed the ground for their sakes and said:

"In the sweat of thy face shalt thou eat bread, till thou return unto the ground; for out of it was thou taken: for dust thou art, and unto dust shalt thou return."(Genesis 3:19)

Mortal Death is Inherited

This mortal death we have inherited, and it is decreed that every soul shall die. However, *it is not the purpose of the Lord that this condition shall endure forever.* Justice demanded that the broken law should be repaired. Death was not to gain the victory. Mankind were not to be forced to partake of everlasting destruction from which there could be no relief. Knowing what Adam would do, the Lord had prepared the way for man's escape from this awful fate. To bring this restoration it was necessary that there could be an infinite atonement that would repair the broken law. It would have been Adam's place to pay the penalty for his transgression; but Adam had placed himself beyond the power by which such an atonement could come. Death had gained a victory over him and likewise over his posterity.

One Without Sin Must Make the Sacrifice

Therefore it became necessary that one who was without sin and free from the power of death, and yet with the power to die, should come to make the sacrifice and redeem mankind from the grave and likewise grant them power of remission of their sins. To fulfill this mission the Son of God was chosen and sent into the world to pay the debt. Peter bears record of this wherein he declared:

"Forasmuch as ye know that ye were not redeemed with corruptible things, as silver and gold, from your vain conversations received by tradition from your fathers: But with the precious blood of Christ, as of a lamb without blemish and without spot;

"Who verily was foreordained before the foundation of the world, but was manifest in these times for you." (I Peter 1:18-20)

Likewise the angel revealed to John in his glorious vision:

"And all that dwell upon the earth shall worship him, whose names are not written in the book of life of the Lamb slain from the foundation of the world."(Rev.13:8)

Paul, in writing to the Church in Corinth taught the atonement of Jesus Christ and the redemption from the grave. Said he:

"If in this life only we have hope in Christ, we are of all men most miserable.

"But now is Christ risen from the dead, and became the first fruits of them that slept.

"For since by man came death, by man came also the resurrection of the dead.

"For as in Adam all die, even so in Christ shall all be made alive.

"But every man in his own order: Christ the firstfruits; afterward they that are Christ's at his coming.

"Then cometh the end, when he shall have delivered up the kingdom of God, even the Father; when he shall have put down all rule and all authority and power.

"For he must reign till he hath put all enemies under his feet.

"The last enemy that shall be destroyed is death.

"For he hath put all things under his feet. But when he saith all things are put under him, it is manifest that he is excepted, which did put all things under him.

"And when all things shall be subdued unto him, then shall the Son also himself be subject unto him that put all things under him, that God may be in all."(I Cor. 15:19-38)

Jesus proclaimed himself to be the "resurrection and the life," (John 11:25) and to the Jews he said:

"For as the Father raiseth up the dead, and quickeneth them; even so the Son quickeneth whom he will.

"Verily, verily, I say unto you, He that heareth my word, and believeth on him that sent me, hath everlasting life, and shall not come into condemnation, but is passed from death unto life.

"Verily, verily, I say unto you. The hour is coming and now is, when the dead shall hear the voice of the Son of God: and they that hear shall live.

"For as the Father hath life in himself; so hath he given to the Son to have life in himself;

"And hath given him authority to execute judgment also, because he is the Son of man.

"Marvel not at this: For the hour is coming, in the which all that are in the graves shall hear his voice.

"And shall come forth; they that have done good, unto the resurrection of life; and they that have done evil, unto the resurrection of damnation."(John 5:21, 24-29)

Again he said to the Jews:

"Even as the Son of man came not to be ministered unto, but to minister and to give his life a ransom for many." (Matt. 20:28)

For God So Loved the World

There is not a more beautiful saying in the Bible than these words of Jesus:

"And as Moses lifted up the serpent in the wilderness, even so must the Son of Man be lifted up;

"That whosoever believeth in him should not perish, but have eternal life.

"For God so loved the world, that he gave his only begotten Son, that whosoever believeth in him should not perish, but have everlasting life.

"For God sent not his Son into the world to comdemn the world; but that the world through him might be saved.

"He that believeth on him is not condemned: but he that believeth not is condemned already, because he hath not believed in the name of the only begotten Son of God.

"And this is the condemnation, that light is come into the world, and men loved darkness rather than light, because their deeds were evil.

"For every one that doeth evil hateth the light, neither cometh to the light, lest his deeds should be reproved.

"But he that doeth truth cometh to the light that his deeds may be made manifest, that they are wrought in God."(John 3:14-21)

No Mortal Could Make the Atonement

The atonement by which men are redeemed, was made by one without blemish and without spot. *He had to be one who had life in himself, and therfore all power over death.* No mortal man could make the atonement. Moreover, *the atonement had to be made by the shedding of blood,* for blood is the vitalizing force of the mortal body. Therefore the Lord said to ancient Israel:

"And whatsoever man there be of the house of Israel, or of the strangers that sojourn among you, that eateth my manner of blood: I will ever set my face against that soul that eateth blood, and will cut him off from among the people.

"For the life of the flesh is in the blood: and I have given it to you upon the altar to make an atonement for your souls: for it is the blood that maketh an atonement for the soul."(Lev.17:10-11)

In Hebrews it is also written:

"And almost all things are by the law purged with blood; and *without shedding of blood is no remission."* (Hebrews 9:22)

The scriptures are replete with passages teaching us that there could be no remission of sins without the shedding of the blood of Jesus Christ. He, when with his apostles at the feast of the last passover, broke and blessed bread and give it to them to eat; likewise he blessed the wine and gave it to them to drink, saying:

"For this is my blood of the testament, which is shed for many for the remission of sins. (Matt. 26:28)

Again to his disciples he said:

"I am the good shepherd, and know my sheep, and am known of mine.

"As the Father knoweth me, even so know I the Father, and I lay down my life for the sheep. . . .

"Therefore doth my Father love me, because I lay down my life that I might take it again.

"No man taketh it from me, but I lay it down of myself. I have power to lay it down, and I have power to take it again. This commandment have I received of my Father."(John 10:14,15,17,18)

The Atonement is Universal

We learn then from these passages that the atonement is universal in its application. And every creature will benefit by it. First, there is a universal redemption from death. It is unconditional. The children of Adam had no agency in the transgression of their first parents, therefore they are not required to exercise any agency in their redemption from its penalty. They are redeemed from death, without faith, repentance, baptism, or any other act, either of mind or of body. These are the dead who have broken the covenants, violated the commandments and who loved darkness rather than light.

The other salvation is that which is given to the righteous, those who confess repentance and a willingness to obey the commandments of God. These are they of whom the Savior spoke, who have "everlasting life," and shall not come into condemnation; but have "passed from death unto life," which life is to dwell in eternal glory. *(CR April 1956, pp.125-127)*

Foundations of the Atonement

Orson Pratt

This discourse was delivered in the new Tabernacle, Salt Lake City, October 7, 1867, during General Conference.

We Come Into the World Innocent

We . . . read that all who come into this world were innocent. That shows that they never had sinned, or if they had that they had been forgiven and made innocent. Which way it was I do not know. If they had sinned and were all made innocent through the blood of the atonement, and through the sufferings of Jesus in the spirit, as well as in the flesh, that would prepare them to come into this world without having any stain upon them. But if they never transgressed the law, never went beyond its bounds, or limits, they would be sanctified, purified, perfected, saved and be innocent by keeping the law. But let us come down a little further. When we came forth into this world, and *took upon ourselves bodies of flesh, they were fallen bodies*—subject to pain, sickness, sorrow, mourning, trials and finally death, or dissolution. This death that came upon the bodies of the children of men, was brought to pass by the transgression of one man and woman, that is, by our first parents; as it is written, "By the transgression of one sin entered the world, and death by sin." It matters not whether it is the little infant that dandles on the knee that has never sinned, or the youth, the middle-aged, or the old, all have to feel this great penalty that has been inflicted upon all the posterity of Adam by reason of his transgression.

Death is Inherited

Now, there is a question that has often been asked of me by the Latter-day Saints, and by those outside of this Church—"Why is it that infants, who have never sinned, should die? Why should they be subject to death because their father some six thousand years ago sinned and transgressed?" I answer this by asking you a question, Why is it that children, oftentimes to the third, fourth, and fifth generation, suffer from lingering diseases here in this life, because their forefathers were licentious and broke the laws of life and happiness? Why, it is hereditary, is it not? Is it just that they should suffer, because their parents or some of their progenitors have sinned? No, it is hereditary. Why, then, may not all the inhabitants of the world, whether in their infancy or not, inherit death as well as these children who suffer through diseases entailed upon them by their forefathers? Not as a matter of justice particularly, but something that comes upon them in consequence of the fall of man. It is handed down among them. Now, that would be a very unpleasant condition if they were always to remain in that state.

Suffering Teaches Experience

They are plunged into slavery, as it were, by one man; hence the Redeemer steps forth and rescues them from that slavery. When I say rescues them, I do not say that he does it at once, before they have had a chance to know the difference between good and evil, between the bitter and the sweet, to contrast between happiness and misery. It is wisdom that they should suffer, even should it be from hereditary disease, that they may gain experience. But I will tell you what he rescues them from, by his atoning blood. He breaks the bands of death and rescues them from the power of the grave, which, but for that, would have held the infant as well as the middle-aged in their power eternally. There is such a thing as a father, through his foolishness, plunging not only himself but all his children into a slavery from which he cannot redeem himself or them, so far as their bodies are concerned; but with Adam's children this was the case with both their bodies and spirits, for the Book of Mormon says that all mankind, through Adam's transgression, became subject not only to a temporal death—the separation of the body and spirit, but also to a spiritual death, eternal in its nature. If there were no atonement—no sufferings and death of our Redeemer—no infinite atonement to rescue men from the grave, their spirits, in consequence of the slavery entailed upon them by their first parents, could not have been rescued from eternal death. Could they have delivered themselves? No. They were in captivity—slavery—and their master, the devil, was there to bind them in that slavery. Could they turn the key of the prison doors and run back again? No! Could they say to the grave, Yield up my body and let me go again into the presence of my Father and God? No; there were potent enemies who had endless power over them had it not been for the atonement.

Christ Suffered the Pain of All Men

We are taught in the revelations of God that Jesus suffered the pain of all men. You will find it in the teachings of Jacob, the brother of Nephi, in the Second book of Nephi. "He suffered the pains of all men, women and children," says Jacob. What was this great suffering for? That the resurrection might come unto all men, women and children; that Jesus might have power to say to the grave "restore those captives you have taken, behold I have redeemed all whose bodies slumber in the grave. I have power to bring them forth by virtue of the atonement I have made."

Man is Under the Power of Satan

Could man have redeemed himself? Could one man have shed his blood for another, and said to the grave give up your dead? No. Why not? Because all were fallen; all were under the dominion and power of Satan. All were spiritually dead—dead to things pertaining to righteousness. It was universal eternal death. A being greater than man was required to redeem him, hence Jacob says, in the passage to which I have already referred, in relation to the atonement, "that it must be infinite."

The Son of God Is Infinite, Immortal

Wherein was the Son of God infinite? In the first place, he was begotten different from you and me. We were begotten by a mortal father, but Jesus was begotten by an Immortal Being, his Father and God. If then his body was begotten by that Being, do you not see that respect differed from ours? It is true that he inherited the same as we do so far as his mother was concerned, but on the part of the Father he was superior. Hence, being begotten by an infinite Being, he could do that which no other man could do—redeem from spiritual death and the captivity of Satan. Hence it is said that "Through Jesus came life and light into the world." If it had not been for Jesus darkness would have reigned eternally over this creation.

Jesus is Our Light and Life

Talk about works of righteousness redeeming us without the atonement! Why the thing is preposterous in the highest degree. Why? Because we were spiritually dead, and can a person who is dead work righteousness? Can a person who is dead to everything good, holy, upright and Godlike, who is in captivity to Satan, work righteousness? Could a feast of salvation be prepared for him in that dead state, unless there was some redemption or atonement made to bring life to the world to impart to the human family? Light and life have come upon all men. Jesus is that light and life: He is the light and life of all things; and by reason of that light and life which he has purchased for us by his own blood, you and I have the privilege of working righteousness, which we never would have had without the atonement. We could not have done anything acceptable in the sight of God, without his atoning blood. That is the very foundation of the redemption of the children of men; without it, this would have been a lost and fallen creation, and not one could have been saved.

* * *

The Plan of Redemption

Now let us come along to the plan of redemption, and see how it is that we are exalted and brought back into the presence of God, and become as it were, gods, then we can form some idea concerning our Father and God. We are instructed, and *we believe, that all of us who believe in Jesus Christ,* in his sufferings and death, and receive the benefit of his atonement, *will, if we remain faithful, be exalted into the presence of that being who is our Father, and that we will be made like unto him,* and be crowned with glory, and shall have the privilege of sitting down with the Son upon his throne, as he has overcome, and has sat down with his Father upon his throne, and that we will become one with him, as he is one with the Father. We believe we will be perfected, purified and cleansed in him, and made not only the sons of God, but grow up unto him in all things, that *we may become Gods like unto our Father who begat us.*

This is consistent with analogy. Analogy shows that sons here upon the earth, grow up and become like their parents. Why then should we set a barrier between the sons of God, who are redeemed through the atonement, and their restoration to the mansions where they formerly dwelt? Why should we erect obstacles, and set a barrier so that we cannot become like him? Analogy would say at once that when he appears we shall be like him, for we shall see him as he is. Analogy would say that when he shall redeem our bodies from the grave, that he will fashion them after his own glorious body, and clothe them with power and glory, even as He is clothed with glory and power, in the presence of his Father and our Father and God. *(JD 19:317-319)*

Absolute Necessity of the Atonement

B. H. Roberts

Elder Roberts made these remarks during General Conference, April, 1911.

A Matter of Faith

I have for many years believed in the atonement of Jesus Christ and have accepted its symbols in baptism and in confirmation; and have repeatedly renewed my acceptance of that atonement by accepting the sacrament of the Lord's Supper. It has been a matter of faith with me and of knowledge, by the testimony of the Spirit to my soul; but upon close inquiry, by deeper delving into the subject my intellect also gives its full and complete assent to the soundness of the philosophy and the absolute necessity for the atonement of Jesus Christ. That this atonement, the method and manner of it is the only way by which there could be brought to pass an at-one-ment, a reuniting of soul of man with soul of God. I account it for myself a new conversion, an intellectual conversion, to the atonement of Jesus Christ; and I have been rejoicing in it of late, exceedingly. I am convinced that when men of intelligence can be brought to the point of being sufficiently humble to read again the Book of Mormon, and to take into account the high purposes for which it was written, viz., to testify to the truth of the Jewish scriptures, but more especially to testify of the Christ, to bear witness of Him both to Jew and Gentile; testifying that Jesus is the Christ, and that there is no other means of salvation provided but through His atonement. When they will consider the message it has to bear upon these important questions, and will stop sneering at such human elements as may be in it, and will examine once more its teachings upon the great theme of salvation through the atonement of the Christ, they can indeed find wisdom and philosophy and truth in its doctrines.

The Atonement Plainly Taught in the Book of Mormon

I proclaim to you, my brethren and sisters, that in the Book of Mormon, more than in any other book written in this world, and I do not except the New Testament—in the Book of Mormon more than in any other book, we have there the necessity of, and the truth of the atonement of the Christ taught to the children of men as nowhere else. I rejoice in these truths; may the Lord seal them upon our hearts and give us grace and strength to live in harmony with them. *(CR April 1911, pp. 58-60)*

Our Very Existence is Dependent On the Atonement

George Q. Morris

Elder Morris was set apart as an Assistant to the Twelve, October, 1951, and was ordained an Apostle April, 1954, and continued to serve the Church in that capacity until his death in April, 1962. Those in attendance at General Conference, April, 1956, heard Elder Morris present this message.

Lehi Expounds the Atonement

I should like to mention in the few moments that I shall be here, something with relation to the atonement, and that it might be fresh in your mind, I wish to read that beautiful statement of Lehi, the great prophet, referring to certain aspects of the atonement:

"And now, behold, if Adam had not transgressed he would not have fallen, but he would have remained in the garden of Eden. And all things which were created must have remained in the same state in which they were after they were created; and they must have remained forever, and had no end.

And they would have had no children; wherefore they would have remained in a state of innocence, having no joy, for they knew no misery; doing no good, for they knew no sin.

"But behold, all things have been done in the wisdom of him who knoweth all things.

"Adam fell that men might be; and men are, that they might have joy." (2 Nephi 2:22-25)

God Desired all to Experience Earth-life

What a wonderful statement that is. So it was the design of our Father in heaven that man should have an earth experience and that Adam should fall and that transgression and sin should come into the world which called for the atonement.

Now, I think the principle question before us is not do we comprehend the atonement, but do we accept it and know that it is true. Many things about us we do not comprehend; as one speaker said, with respect to electricity, the scientific men say they do not know all about it, do not know much about it, they do not know what it is. They know how it acts, but they do not know why it acts, and yet we all avail ourselves of the blessing of electricity without comprehending it.

Without the Atonement, all is Vain

I think it is exactly the same with the glorious principle of atonement. If electricity in our highly developed civilization were taken out of our lives, our civilization would stop, it is so integrated into our activities. And if the principle of the atonement were taken away, what would be the result? We would have no Jewish scriptures, we would have no Jewish people. There would have been no covenant with Abraham. We would have no New Testament. We would have no gospel of Jesus Christ, for the atonement is the foundation of it all.

And what would spirit world existence mean, what objective would it have, if there were nothing beyond your existence in the spirit world, because God found it necessary for us to come to the earth to get our experience, to gain a body, to pass through death, to be raised an immortalized and glorified being so that we might go on to perfection. Without the atonement there would have been no creation of an earth because that would have meant that we would have all come to the earth as is stated by Lehi, and after transgression had occurred, death would follow, and the earth would be merely the eternal graveyard of the sons and daughters of God. That would have been the end.

The Lord would not undertake to create an earth for that end. An earth life would never have been planned except for this glorious principle of the atonement. And would we have an heaven without the principle of the atonement, would we ever have had an existence in heaven as spirit children of God without the atonement, for God the Eternal Father is a being, a Glorified Being of flesh and bone, exalted and celestialized, and that comes through death and the resurrection by means of the atonement. Unless spirit and matter are inseparably connected, we cannot have a fulness of joy. And if they are so connected, we may have joy in its fullest degree, which I would say means attainment, achievement, exaltation. We must come to the earth; we must have earth life; we must go through death; and we must be exalted and glorified through the power of God and through the gospel and the resurrection.

We Need not Comprehend the Atonement to Know It

None of these things would have been possible or comtemplated or planned or carried out without this glorious principle of atonement, the Son of God dying for all the children of men. We may not be able to comprehend it, in its fulness, but we can know it, and we can understand how the Son of God, the Firstborn among all the children of God, dying for all the rest, would gain power and influence over the children of men, and we can understand what their devotion should be towards him because his suffering was such that no human being could endure it. He accepted it. It was so terrible that he almost wished that he might not have to endure it. But he accepted it and glorified his Father in heaven and made possible our earth life, our resurrection, our exaltation, and the blessings of eternal life. *(CR April 1956, pp.112-113)*

An Infinite Atonement

John Taylor

This selection is excerpted from President Taylor's book, The Mediation and Atonement.

Christ Could Not Do For Others What He Could Not Do For Himself

In the economy of God pertaining to the salvation of the human family, we are told in the Scriptures that it was necessary that Christ should descend below all things, that He might be raised above all things; . . . He had to "become subject to man in the flesh." *It was further necessary that He should descend below all things, in order that He might raise others above all things;* for if He could not raise Himself and be exalted through those principles brought about by the atonement, He could not raise others; He could not do for others what He could not do for Himself, and hence it was necessary for Him to descend below all things that He might be raised above all things; and it was necessary that those whom He proposed to save should also descend below all things, that by and through the same power that He obtained His exaltation, they also, through His atonement, expiation and intercession, might be raised to the same power with Him; and, as He was the Son of God, that they might also be the adopted sons of God; hence John says:

"Beloved, now are we the sons of God; and it doth not yet appear what we shall be: but we know that, when he shall appear, we shall be like him; for we shall see him as he is." (I John 3:2)

And by this power we shall overcome and sit down on His throne, as Jesus overcame and sat down upon the throne of His Father.

The Atonement Must Be Infinite

We are told . . . that the atonement must needs be infinite. Why did it need an infinite atonement? For the simple reason that a *stream can never rise higher than its fountain;* and man having assumed a fleshly body and become of the earth earthy, and through the violation of a law having cut himself off from his association with his Father, and become subject to death; in this condition, as the mortal life of man was short, and in and of himself he could have no hope of benefiting himself, or redeeming himself from his fallen condition, or of bringing himself back to the presence of his Father, some superior agency was needed to elevate him above his low and degraded position. This superior agency was the Son of God, who had not, as man had, violated a law of His Father, but was yet one with His Father, possessing His glory, His power, His authority, His dominion. As He, Himself, prayed:

"And now, O Father, glorify thou me with thine own self, with the glory which I had with thee before the world was." (John 17:5)

Joint Heirs with Christ

A man, as a man, could arrive at all the dignity that a man was capable of obtaining or receiving; but it needed a God to raise him to the dignity of a God. For this cause it is written, "Now are we the sons of God; and it doth not yet appear what we shall be: but we know that when he shall appear we shall be like him." And how and why like Him? Because, through the instrumentality of the atonement and the adoption, it is made possible for us to become of the family of God, and joint heirs with Jesus Christ; and that as He, the potential instrument, through the oneness that existed between Him and His Father, by reason of obedience to divine law, overcame death, hell and the grave, and sat down upon His Father's throne, so shall we be able to sit down with Him, even upon His throne. Thus, as it is taught in the Book of Mormon, it must needs be that there be an infinite atonement; and hence of Him, and by Him, and through Him are all things; and *through Him do we obtain every blessing, power, right, immunity, salvation and exaltation.* He is our God, our Redeemer, our Savior, to whom, with the Father and the Holy Spirit, be eternal and everlasting praises, worlds without end.

(The Mediation and Atonement, pp. 144-146)

Universal Redemption

Orson Pratt

The following has been taken from a much longer discourse, delivered by Elder Pratt.

In the Beginning Immortality Reigned

The earth was formed to be inhabited—it was designed to be the abode of animated existence—the dwelling place of beings capable of enjoying life and happiness.

* * *

Here immortality reigned, and death had no dominion. The elements were so wisely arranged and proportioned, that life was derived from all things ordained for the use of man or beast, fowl or fish. . . . Death was unknown; it had not been seen, heard of, nor experienced in all the varied ranks of earthly beings.

Here, then, was a creation "very good," inhabited by beings capable of eternal existence, both body and spirit. Here was a creation adapted to the wants of all its inhabitants, calculated to preserve unchanged that immortality with which they were endowed. Here, then, was a creation worth possessing as an eternal abode.

Man Broke the Law and Fell

Such was the inheritance given to man, with its vast treasures and sumptuous luxuries—such was the gift of heaven under certain restrictions. These restrictions were not complied with—man fell—a great change came over the fair face of creation—*the earth was cursed—sickness, pain, and misery ensued*—immortality yielded to mortality—*death reigned triumphantly* throughout the animal kingdom—the everlasting inheritance on the newly-formed earth was forfeited—all seemed to be lost—forever lost! While all creation groaned in utter despair and death, a voice was heard; not a voice of wrath and indignation, but the voice of mercy and compassion—the voice of the Creator, proclaiming himself the Redeemer; love flowed through every sentence—man listened with eagerness—the door of hope was opened—despair fled away—all things again assumed a new aspect. The earth, though cursed, was to be redeemed—the body, though corruptible, was again to put on incorruption—all things lost by the first transgression were to be restored again in their primitive excellence and beauty.

Redemption—A Gradual Change

Though this great redemption was to be universal, yet the change was to be gradual or progressive, not immediate; the effects of the fall were to continue for a season, until all the inhabitants of the spirit world, designed for this creation, should learn by bitter experience, the unhappy consequences of sin. Hence, the whole world still groans under the sad effects of the original transgression. Sorrow, mourning, and death, still prevail—the aged, middle-aged, and infant still feel the force of these evils—all are made partakers in a greater or less degree of wretchedness and miseries of the fall—none escape—none can proclaim themselves immortal, or free from these direful effects.

The Redemption Will Be Completed After All Have Been Resurrected

The universal redemption of the posterity of Adam from the fall will be fully accomplished after the earth has been filled with its measure of inhabitants, and all men have been redeemed from the grave to immortality, and the earth itself has been changed and made entirely new.

But a *universal redemption* from the effects of original sin has *nothing to do with redemption from our personal sins;* for the original sin of Adam, and the personal sins of his children, are two different things. The first was committed by man in his immortal state; the second was committed by man in a mortal state; the former was committed in a state of ignorance of good or evil; the latter was committed by man, having a knowledge of both good and evil.

The Penalties Are Different For Different Sins

As the sins are different, and committed entirely under different circumstances, so the penalties are different also. The penalty of the first transgression was an eternal separation of body and spirit, and eternal banishment from the presence of Jehovah; while the penalty of our own transgressions does not involve a disunion of body and spirit, but only eternal banishment. *The first penalty not only shut man out from the presence of God, but deprived him eternally of a body; the second penalty permits him to retain his body, though in a banished condition.* As the penalties are different, so also is the redemption.

Unconditional Versus Conditional Redemption

Redemption from the first penalty is unconditional on the part of man; redemption from the second penalty is conditional. Unconditional redemption is universal; it takes within its scope all mankind; it is as unlimited as the fall; it redeems men from all its effects; it restores them to their bodies; it restores them to the presence of God.

The children of Adam had no agency in the transgression of their first parents, and therefore *they are not required to exercise any agency in their redemption from its penalty.* They are redeemed from it without faith, repentance, baptism, or any other act, either of the mind or body.

* * *

The Earth to be Redeemed Unconditionally

The earth, like the posterity of Adam, was cursed because of original sin, and like them, it will be redeemed unconditionally, and restored again into the presence of God. So far as the original sin is concerned, mankind and the earth keep pace with each other. When one falls, the other falls also. When one is redeemed, the other is redeemed also.

Had there been no other sin but that of Adam's, the redeemed earth would have become the eternal abode of all the posterity of Adam, without one exception. *(JD 1:328-330)*

Man and The Atonement

Orson Pratt

The Journal of Discourses prefaces this selection as "A General Funeral Sermon of all Saints and Sinners; also, of the Heavens and the Earth." It was delivered in the old Tabernacle in Salt Lake City, July 25, 1852.

All Must Undergo the Penalty of Death

In order to show you the dire effects of the fall, it is not only necessary to say that old father Adam has experienced that penalty, and laid down his body in the dust; but all generations since that time have experienced the same; and you, and I, and every man, and woman, and child, have got to undergo that penalty; it will be inflicted upon us, and thus will the law of God be magnified, His words fulfilled, and justice have its demands. *It is not because of our sins, that we die;* it is not because we have transgressed, that we die; it is not because we may commit murder, or steal, or plunder, or rob, or take the name of the Lord in vain; it is not these things that bring the death of the body; *but it is Adam's sin* that makes the little child die, that makes kings, princes, and potentates die, and *that has made all the generations die from his day down to the present time.* Don't you think there ought to be some way to redeem us from this dreadful calamity? We had no hand in the transgression of Adam; you and I were not there to participate in it; but it was our great father who did it, and we are suffering the effects of it.

Physicians Cannot Relieve Us From Death

Cannot some of the wise medical men of the age—some of the great physicians and doctors of the day, who have studied medicine all their life—can they not imagine up something new, that will relieve the posterity of Adam from this awful calamity? They have not done it yet. Dr. Brandreth recommended his medicine for all kinds of diseases, and even it was said that steam-boats were propelled by its power; but it made no man immortal; it did not save one man; and it is doubtful in the extreme—it is certain, that no man in this mortality has ever discovered that medicine which will relieve us from these awful effects transmitted from father Adam to this present time.

The Only Remedy Comes From God

There is a remedy, but it is not to be found in the catalogue of inventions of man; it is not to be found in the bowels of the earth, or dug out of any mines; it is not to be purchased by the gold of California, or the treasures of India. What is it, and how was it discovered? *It was the Being who made man,* that made him immortal and eternal, that Being whose bosom is filled with mercy, as well as justice, that exercises both attributes, and shows to all creation that He is a merciful God, as well as a God of justice; it was He *that discovered this wonderful remedy to preserve mankind from the effects of this eternal death.* But when is it to be applied? Not immediately, for that would frustrate His designs: when the body has got back into the dust, and after man has suffered sufficiently long for the original sin, He then brings him forth to enjoy all the bloom of immortality; He tells Death to trouble him no more; He wipes away all tears from his eyes, for he is prepared to live forever, and gaze upon His glory, and dwell in His presence.

The Great Redeemer is Stronger Than Death

This great Redeemer is stronger than Death, more powerful than that direful monster who has come into the world, and laid seige to all the inhabitants thereof; He will banish it out of his creation. How will He do it? If the penalty of the original sin be the eternal separation of body and spirit, how can justice have all its demands, and mercy be shown to the transgressor? There is a way, and how? It is by the introduction of His Only Begotten Son, the Son of His own bosom, the first-born of every creature, holding the birthright over every creation He has made, and holding the keys of salvation over millions of worlds like this; he has a right to come forth and suffer the penalty of death for the fallen sons and daughters of man. He offered his own life: says He, *"Father, I will suffer death, though I have not merited it; let me suffer the demands of the law.* Here I am innocent in thy presence; I have always kept thy laws from the day of my birth among thy creations, throughout ages past down to the present time; I have never been rebellious to thy commandments; and now *I will suffer for my brethren and sisters:*let thy justice be magnified and made honourable; here am I; let me suffer the ends of the law, and *let death and the grave deliver up their victims,* and *let the posterity of Adam all be set free,* every soul of them without an exception." This is the way that justice is magnified and made honourable, and none of the creations of the Almighty can complain of Him, that He has not answered the ends of justice;

no intelligent being can say, "You have deviated from your words." Justice has had its demands in the penalties that were inflicted upon the Son of God, so far as Adam's transgression is concerned.

Each Man, Woman and Child to be Redeemed From the Original Sin

I will explain a little further. So far as that transgression is concerned, all the inhabitants of the earth will be saved. Now understand me correctly. If there are any strangers present, that have not understood the views of the Latter-day Saints, I wish you to understand that *we have no reference in any way to your own personal sins;* but so far as the original sin of father Adam is concerned, you and I will have to suffer death; and every man and woman that ever lived on this globe will be redeemed from that sin. On what condition? I answer, on no condition whatever on our part. "But," says one, "where I came from they tell me I ought to repent for the original sin." I care not what they tell you, *you will be redeemed from the original sin, with no works on your part whatever.* Jesus has died to redeem you from it, and you are as sure to be redeemed, as you live upon the face of this earth. This is the kind of universal redemption the "Mormons" believe in, though in one sense of the word, it is a different kind of universal redemption from that which the nations have been in the habit of hearing. We believe in the universal redemption of all the children of Adam into the presence of God, so far as the sins of Adam are concerned. They will obtain a universal redemption from the grave. It matters not how wicked you are; if you have murdered all the days of your life, and committed all the sins the devil would prompt you to commit, you will get a resurrection; your spirit will be restored to your body. If Jesus had not come, all of us would have slumbered in the grave; but now, wicked as we may be, if we go down to the grave blaspheming the name of the Lord, we shall as sure come up again as we go down there. This is free grace without works; all this comes to pass without works on the part of the creature.

***

All Must be Judged For Their Own works

After you have been redeemed from the grave, and come into the presence of God, you will have to stand there to be judged; and if you have done evil, you will be banished everlastingly from His presence—body and spirit united together; this is what is called the second death.

***

There is a way of escape from the effects of your own individual transgressions, but it is different from the redemption from the original sin of Adam. The redemption from that sin was universal without works, but the redemption from your own personal sins is universal with works on the part of the creature—universal in its nature, because it is free to all, but not received by all. The salvation, or redemption from your own sins, is not be free grace alone, it requires a little work. But what are the works? Jesus Christ, through his death and sufferings, has answered the penalty, on condition that you believe in him and *repent of your sins, and be baptized for the remission of them, and receive the gift of the Holy Ghost, by the laying on of hands,* and continue humble, and meek, and prayerful, until you go down to your graves; and on these conditions, Jesus will plead for you before the Father, and say, "Father, I not only died for Adam's sin, but for the sins of all the world, inasmuch as they believe in my Gospel; and now these individuals have repented, they have reformed their lives, and have become like little children in my sight, and have performed the works I have given them to do—and now, Father, may they be saved with an everlasting salvation in thy presence, and sit down with me on my throne, as I have overcome, and sit down with thee on thy throne; and may they be crowned with all the sanctified, with immortality and eternal life, no more to be cast away."

Jesus Christ is Our Mediator with God

Don't you think the Father would accept an appeal of this kind from His Only Begotten Son? Yes. He is our Mediator, to plead before the Father for those who will comply with his commands, and the laws of his Gospel. The way is simple, so simple and easy that many step over it and say, "O, that is of no consequence, it is of no avail, it will do no good to be baptized in water." But if the Lord had not constructed it upon a simple plan, adapted to the capacities of all men, they might have had some excuse; but as it is, they have none: *all you have got to do is to believe that Jesus Christ is the Son of God, turn away from your sins, cease to do evil,* saying, "Father, I will cease from this time henceforth to sin, and will work the works of righteousness; I will try to do good all the days of my life; and I witness this before thee by this day going down into the waters of baptism; and thus cast off the old man, with his deeds," and henceforth live in newness of life. If you will do this, you will just as sure be redeemed from your own sins and the penalty thereof, and be lifted up to dwell in the presence of God, as you have been redeemed or lifted up from the waters of baptism.

(JD 1:286-289)

Heirs of Godhood

John Taylor

Once again we excerpt from President Taylor's, The Mediation and Atonement.

The Atonement was Instituted for the Exaltation of Man

The philosophy of the world tells us that the spirit dies with the body, and like it is dissipated in surrounding nature, but as an entirety no longer exists; and all the power the being ever had was to propagate its own species and to impart the powers of the body and the mind to its posterity. Such philosophers can comprehend nothing pertaining to the future—no glory, no exaltation, no eternal progression, only as developed by a succession of manhood. If, then, there is a spirit in man which reaches into futurity, that would grasp eternal progress, eternal enjoyments, and eternal exaltations; then those glories, those exaltations, those capabilities and those powers must be the gift of some superior being, power, or authority to that which exists in man; for the foregoing is a brief exhibition of the powers and capabilities of humanity. It is of this gift that we now speak. It is of a principle that emanates from God, that originates with a superior intelligence, whose plans, and powers, and capabilities are exalted above those of mortal man, as the heavens are above the earth, or as the majestic works of the Great Creator throughout the infinitude of space are superior to the puny efforts of the children of mortality. It is for the exaltation of man to this state of superior intelligence and Godhead that the mediation and atonement of Jesus Christ is instituted; and that noble being, man, made in the image of God, is rendered capable not only of being a son of man, but also a son of God, through adoption, and is rendered capable of becoming a God, possessing the power, the majesty, the exaltation and the position of a God. As it is written, "Beloved, now are we the sons of God; and it doth not yet appear what we shall be; but we know that, when he shall appear, we shall be like him; for we shall see him as he is."

Man Can Rise to the Dignity of a God

As a man through the powers of his body he could attain to the dignity and completeness of manhood, but could go no further; as a man he is born, as a man he lives, and as a man he dies; but through the essence and power of the Godhead, which is in him, which descended to him as the gift of God from his heavenly Father, he is capable of rising from the contracted limits of manhood to the dignity of a God, and thus through the atonement of Jesus Christ and the adoption he is capable of eternal exaltation, eternal lives and eternal progression. But this transition from his manhood to the Godhead can alone be made through a power which is superior to man—an infinite power, an eternal power, even the power of the Godhead: for as in Adam all die, so in Christ *only* can all be made alive. Through Him mankind are brought into communion and communication with God; through His atonement they are enabled, as He was, to vanquish death; through that atonement and the power of the Priesthood associated therewith, they become heirs of God and joint heirs with Jesus Christ, and inheritors of thrones, powers, principalities and dominions in the eternal worlds. And instead of being subject to death, when that last enemy shall be destroyed, and death be swallowed up in victory, through that atonement they can become the fathers and mothers of lives, and be capable of perpetual and eternal progression.

(The Mediation and Atonement, pp. 140-141)

Only Deity Can Satisfy the Claims of Deity

B. H. Roberts

This selection is taken from "The Seventy's Course in Theology, Fourth Year" by Elder Roberts.

A Sin Against the Majesty of God

The sin of Adam was a sin against divine law; a sin against the majesty of God. *Only a God can render a satisfaction to that insulted honor and majesty.* Only Deity can satisfy the claims of Deity.

And hence Alma says, in speaking of the Atonement, and in view of the inadequacy of any atonement man himself can make: "It shall not be a human sacrifice; but *it must be an infinite and eternal sacrifice. . . .* And behold, this is the whole meaning of the law; every whit pointing to that great and last sacrifice; and that great and last sacrifice will be the Son of God; yea, infinite and eternal . . . The plan of mercy could not be brought about except an atonement should be made; therefore God himself atoneth for the sins of the world to bring about the plan of Mercy, to appease the demands of Justice." (Alma 34:10-14, 42:15; see also 2 Nephi 9:7)

Power Over Death

Moreover the Atonement is not only a matter of satisfying the insulted honor and majesty of God adequately by like meeting like, and measure answering measure; but it is also a question of power. Not only must the dishonor towards God be removed by a satisfaction, but there must be power over death; there must be a power of life that that which was lost may be restored; and not only as the spiritual life of man with God; but restored union between the spirit and body of man—physical life upon which the happiness and progress that God has designed for man depends. "Man," it should always be remembered, "is spirit." "The elements (meaning elements of matter) are eternal; and spirit and element inseparably connected receive a fulness of joy." (D&C 93:33, 34) Hence the importance of man's physical life, the union of his deathless spirit with a body that must be made equally immortal; and since the fall brought to man this physical death as well as the spiritual death; his redemption, to be complete, must re-establish that physical life by reuniting the essential elements of the body of man and his spirit, in the resurrection, and the resurrection must be universal; *the Atonement in its redeeming effects must be as universal as the fall.* As in Adam all die, so through the Redeemer of men must all be made alive, if the redemption is to be complete. It was doubtless these considerations which led some of the Nephite prophets to say that the Atonement "must needs be an infinite atonement;" by which, as I think, they sought to express the idea of the sufficiency of it; its completeness; the universality and power of it to restore all that was lost, both spiritual and physical, as well as to express the rank and dignity of him who would make the Atonement.

The Redeemer is the Lord of Life

The Redeemer, then, must be a Lord of life, hence Deity. He must not only have the power of life within himself, but the power to impart it to others—a God-like power; and to inspire faith in his possession of such power, the manner of the Atonement must be such as to include demonstration of that fact, else how shall men have faith in him? All these considerations lift the Redeemer and the Atonement far above man and what man can do. Truly *the redemption of man is to be the work of God.*

And now for the scripture warrant for these conclusions:

"I lay down my life for the sheep [men] . . . Therefore doth my Father love me, because I lay down my life, that I might take it again. No man taketh it from me, but I lay it down of myself. *I have power to lay it down, and I have Power to take it again.* This commandment have I received of my Father." (John 10:17,18)

"Destroy this temple and in three days I will raise it up; . . .he spake of the temple of his body, when therefore he was risen from the dead, his disciples remembered that he had said this unto them." (John 2:19-22) "Thus it behooved Christ to suffer, and to rise from the dead the third day." (Luke 24:46)

"In him was life; and the life was the light of men. Verily, verily I say unto you, The Son can do nothing of himself, but what he seeth the Father do; for what things soever he doeth, these also doeth the Son likewise. For the Father loveth the Son, and sheweth him all things that himself doeth; and he will shew him greater works than these, that ye may marvel. For as the Father raiseth up the dead, and quickeneth them; even so the Son quickeneth whom he will." (John 5:19-21)

"Verily, verily, I say unto you, the hour is coming and now is when the dead shall hear the voice of the Son of God; and they that hear shall live. For as the Father hath life in himself so hath he given to the Son to have life in himself; and hath given him authority to execute judgment also, because he is the Son of man. Marvel not at this; for the hour is coming, in which all that are in graves shall hear his voice. And shall come forth; they that have done good, unto the resurrection of life; and they that have done evil, unto the resurection of damnation." (John 5:25-29)

God Himself Must Redeem Man

But to return now to the thought that God himself must make atonement for man's transgression. And we come back to that thought with increased conviction after considering the necessary element of power in connection with the Atonement, the ability to restore that which was lost—life, spiritual and physical; not the work of man, but the work of a Deity, a Lord of life—God must himself redeem man. That or justice must take its course and the sinner be left to satisfy the justice of God by an endless misery under the sentence of law; without union with God—spiritual death; and subject to the dissolution of spirit and body, without the power of resurrection—physical death. But that would thwart the purpose of God with reference to the earth-life of man, which was designed for his progress, that progress might bring him joy. Moreover, to leave man under the penalty of a broken law, which means to him eternal death, physical and spiritual, would be contrary to the pledge of eternal life "which God, that cannot lie, promised before the world began."

(Titus 1:1,2) Under these circumstances justice may not be left to take its course. *There must be an atonement made for man and as none but God can make an adequate atonement in the case, then a Deity must make it.* And hence, one of the Nephite prophets, coming to the same conclusion, wrote:"And now the plan of mercy could not be brought about, except an atonement should be made; therefore God himself atoneth for the sins of the world, to bring about the plan of mercy, to appease the demands of justice, that God might be a perfect, just God, and a merciful God also."

A Sacrifice Without Spot or Blemish

The Atonement, we conclude, must be made by a Deity, in order to be adequate; but it must be made by a Deity living in a man's life—hence the incarnation of the spirit of a Deity in the person of Jesus Christ. It must be made by a Deity who will live man's life with all its temptations, yet remain without sin that the sacrifice might be without spot or blemish; by one who will give to the world the illustration and the one demonstration of a perfect life—a life in which the will is wholly subjected to the will of God. Also *the Atonement must be made by a Deity living man's life* that the satisfaction to the justice of God may be rendered from the same plane on which the offense was offered, and essentially from amid the same conditions. Hence the special temptation of Jesus by Lucifer. The *Atonement must be made by a Deity who shall die man's death,* but who shall not be holden of it, but break its bands and demonstrate the power of the resurrection of which he is the first fruits, and ever after Lord of life and the power of the resurrection—such, for instance, as was Jesus Christ.

(The Seventy's Course in Theology, Fourth Year, 1911, pp. 94-97)

He Bore the Sins of the World

John Taylor

The following is taken from The Mediation and Atonement *by President Taylor.*

"Suffer Little Children to Come Unto Me"

The Redeemer Himself, when tabernacling in the flesh, said to His disciples on the Eastern Continent, "Suffer little children to come unto me, and forbid them not: for of such is the kingdom of

God. Verily I say unto you, Whosoever shall not receive the kingdom of God as a little child shall in no wise enter therein." (Luke 18:16,17) And after His crucifixion and resurrection, He repeated this same admonition to His Nephite disciples: "And again I say unto you, Ye must repent, and be baptized in my name and become as a little child, or ye can in no wise inherit the kingdom of God." (3 Nephi 11:38)

Without Adam's transgression those children could not have existed; through the atonement they are placed in a state of salvation without any act of their own. These would embrace, according to the opinion of statisticians, more than one-half of the human family, who can attribute their salvation only to the mediation and atonement of the Savior. Thus, as stated elsewhere, in some mysterious, incomprehensible way, *Jesus assumed the responsibility which naturally would have devolved upon Adam;* but which could only be accomplished through the mediation of Himself, and by taking upon Himself their sorrows, assuming their responsibilities, and bearing their transgressions or sins.

He Bore the Weight of the Sins of the World

In a manner to us incomprehensible and inexplicable, he bore the weight of the sins of the whole world; *not only of Adam but of his posterity;* and in doing that, opened the kingdom of heaven, not only to all believers and all who obeyed the law of God, but to more than one-half of the human family who die before they come to years of maturity, as well as to the heathen, who, having died without law, will, through His mediation, be resurrected without law, and be judged without law, and thus participate, according to their capacity, works and worth, in the blessings of His atonement.

Without Shedding of Blood there is No Remission

Again, there is another phase of this subject that must not be forgotten. From the commencement of the offering of sacrifices the inferior creature had to suffer for the superior. Although it had taken no part in the act of disobedience, yet was its blood shed and its life sacrificed, thus prefiguring the atonement of the Son of God, which should eventually take place. The creature indeed was made subject to vanity not willingly, but by reason of Him who hath subjected the same in hope. Millions of such offerings were made, and hecatombs of these expiatory sacrifices were offered in view of the great event that would be consummated when Jesus should offer up Himself. With man this was simply the obedience to a command and a given law, and with him might be considered simply a pecuniary sacrifice: with the animals it was a sacrifice of life. But what is the reason for all this suffering and bloodshed, and sacrifice? We are told that "without shedding of blood is no remission" of sins. This is beyond our comprehension. *Jesus had to take away sin by the sacrifice of Himself,* the just for the unjust, but, previous to this grand sacrifice, these animals had to have their blood shed as types, until the great antetype should offer up Himself once for all. And as He in His own person bore the sins of all, and atoned for them by the sacrifice of Himself, so there came upon Him the weight and agony of ages and generations, the indescribable agony consequent upon this great sacrificial atonement wherein He bore the sins of the world, and suffered in His own person the consequences of an eternal law of God broken by man. Hence His profound grief, His indescribable anguish, His overpowering torture, all experienced in the submission to the eternal fiat of Jehovah and requirements of an inexorable law.

The Suffering of Christ is an Incomprehensible Burden

The suffering of the Son of God was not simply the suffering of personal death; for in assuming his position that He did in making an atonement for the sins of the world He bore the weight, the responsibility, and the burden of the sins of all men, which, to us, is incomprehensible. As stated, "the Lord, your Redeemer, suffered death in the flesh; wherefore he suffereth the pains of all men;" and Isaiah says: "Surely he hath borne our griefs and carried our sorrows," also, "The Lord hath laid on him the iniquity of us all," and again, "He hath poured out his soul unto death, and he has numbered with the transgressors: and he bare the sins of many;" or, as it is written in the Second Book of Nephi: "For behold, *he suffered the pains* of all men; yea, the pains *of every living creature,* both men, women and children, who belong to the family of Adam;" whilst in Mosiah it is declared: "He shall suffer temptations, and pain of body, hunger, thirst and fatigue, even more than man can suffer, except it be unto death; for behold, blood cometh from every pore, so great shall be his anguish for the wickedness and abominations of his people."

"Let This Cup Pass From Me."

Groaning beneath this concentrated load, this intense, incomprehensible pressure, this terrible exaction of Divine justice, from which feeble humanity shrank, and through the agony thus experienced sweating great drops of blood, He was led to exclaim, "Father, if it be possible, let this cup pass from me." He had wrestled with the superincumbent load in the wilderness, He had struggled against the powers of darkness that had been let loose upon him there; placed below all things, His mind surcharged with agony and pain, lonely and apparently helpless and forsaken, in his agony the blood oozed from His pores. Thus rejected by His own, attacked by the powers of darkness, and seemingly forsaken by His God, on the cross He bowed beneath the accumulated load, and cried out in anguish, "My God, my God, why hast thou forsaken me!"When death approached to relieve Him from His horrible position, a ray of hope appeared through the abyss of darkness with which He had been surrounded, and in a spasm of relief, seeing the bright future beyond, He said, "It is finished! Father, into thy hands I commend my spirit."

He Vanquished Death

*As a God, He descended below all things, and made Himself subject to man in man's fallen condition:*as a man, He grappled with all the circumstances incident to His sufferings in the world. Anointed, indeed, with the oil of gladness above His fellows, *He struggled with and overcame the powers of men and devils, of earth and hell combined;* and aided by this superior power of the God-head, He vanquished death, hell and the grave, and arose triumphant as the Son of God, the very eternal Father, the Messiah, the Prince of peace, the Redeemer, the savior of the world; having finished and completed the work pertaining to the atonement, which His Father had given Him to do as the Son of God and the Son of man. *As the Son of Man, He endured all that it was possible for flesh and blood to endure; as the Son of God He triumphed over all, and forever ascended to the right hand of God,* to further carry out the designs of Jehovah pertaining to the world and to the human family.

(The Mediation and Atonement,pp. 148-151)

The Sacrifice

"For God so loved the world, that he gave his only begotten Son, that whosoever believeth in him should not perish, but have everlasting life."
(John 3:16)

A Supreme Sacrifice

Rudger Clawson

Elder Clawson was ordained an Apostle October, 1898, and was called as Second Counselor to President Lorenzo Snow on October 6, 1901. He was released four days later when President Snow died, never having been set apart in that calling. He returned to his position in the Quorum of Twelve Apostles and became president of that Quorum March 17, 1921, and served until his death in June, 1943. His remarks here were delivered to General Conference, October, 1921.

A Similitude of the Sacrifice of the Son of God

The Lord Jesus Christ has wrought out for us a great salvation by the shedding of blood. The atonement is many times referred to in the holy scriptures of both the Old and the New Testament; and, in fact, in the very beginning this important matter was emphasized. When Adam and Eve were thrust out of the Garden of Eden, the Lord commanded them to worship him and to offer the firstlings of their flock upon an altar of sacrifice. Adam was obedient to the commandment. Later an angel appeared to him and asked him why he was offering sacrifice, and he answered and said: "I know now, only that the Lord commanded it." And then it was that the angel explained the matter in very striking language. This is what he said, as recorded in the Pearl of Great Price:

"This thing is a similitude of the sacrifice of the Only Begotten Son of the Father, which is full of grace and truth. Wherefore thou *shalt do all that thou doest in the name of the Son,* and thou shalt repent and call upon God in the name of the Son forever."

The Offering of Abraham

Isaac was offered upon an altar of sacrifice by his father Abraham, and it seems that this was intended to test his faith and obedience. He readily responded, but the Lord would not suffer him to lay his hand upon the boy. Surely this offering of Abraham was typical of the great offering made by God himself, for it is said in the record that, God so loved the world that he gave his Only Begotten Son that whosoever believeth in him should not perish, but have everlasting life.

Burnt Offerings of the Children of Israel

Let me remind you that there was a deep significance in the burnt offerings of the children of Israel in the wilderness and in Palestine, because *it was through these burnt offerings that the children of Israel obtained forgiveness of their sins,* for the burnt offerings were typical of the great atonement that would be made by the Lamb of God in later years.

Isaiah Spoke of the Atonement

Isaiah, the Prophet, that mighty man of ancient times, speaks of the atonement in a very beautiful and expressive manner. Listen to the language of the Seer:

"But he was wounded for our transgressions, he was bruised for our iniquities; the chastisement of our peace was upon him; and with his stripes we are healed.

"All we like sheep have gone astray; we have turned every one to his own way; and the Lord hath laid on him the iniquity of us all . . .

"He was taken from prison and from judgment: and who shall declare his generations? for he was cut off out of the land of the living: for the transgression of my people was he stricken . . .

"He shall see of the travail of his soul, and shall be satisfied: by his knowledge shall my righteous servant justify many; for he shall bear their iniquities.

"Therefore will I divide him a portion with the great, and he shall divide the spoil with the strong; because he hath poured out his soul unto death; and he was numbered with the transgressors; and he bare the sin of many, and made intercession for the transgressors."

And the subject is also referred to in the book of Revelation, in chapter five, where reference is made to the Savior of the world:

"And they sung a new song, saying, Thou are worthy to take the book, and to open the seals thereof: for thou wast slain, and hast redeemed us to God by thy blood out of every kindred, and tongue, and people and nation."

In the meridian of time the Lord required of his people a broken heart and a contrite spirit, and he introduced the sacrament saying:

"And the Lord took the bread and gave thanks and blessed it, and he gave unto them saying: This is my body which is given for you. This do in remembrance of me."

"Likewise also the cup after supper, saying: This cup is the new testament in my blood which is shed for you."

The Lord Requires a Broken Heart and a Contrite Spirit

And so, my brethren and sisters, it is in the dispensation of the fulness of times, for the Lord requires of us a broken heart and a contrite spirit, and the sacrament, which is regarded by the Church as a most holy ordinance, is again restored to the people of God. We are commanded to come together often and partake of the sacrament, in remembrance of him, of his suffering and death. Oh, how important is this subject. Again in one of the great revelations of the Lord to the Prophet Joseph Smith, and to the people of the Church, the Lord refers to this subject in a most touching and beautiful manner. Give ear, brethren and sisters, to these words which were uttered by revelation, in 1831:

"Hearken, O ye people of my Church to whom the kingdom has been given. Hearken ye and give ear to him who laid the foundations of the earth; who made the heavens and all the hosts thereof, and by whom all things were made which live and move and have their being. And again I say, hearken unto my voice, least death shall overtake you in an hour when you think not, and summer shall be past and the harvest ended and your souls not saved. Listen to him who is the advocate with the Father, who is pleading your cause before him, saying: Father behold the sufferings and death of him who did no sin in whom thou wast well pleased. Behold the blood of thy Son which was shed, the blood of him whom thou gavest that thyself might be glorified. Wherefore, Father, spare these my brethren that believe on my name, that they may come unto me and have everlasting life."

An Obligation Which can Never be Repaid

These passages which I have read, and many more that occur in the Holy Scriptures, give us to understand that the atonement made upon Mount Calvary was the supreme sacrifice ever made in all the world. Oh, the height and the depth of divine love, the love of God for his children here upon the earth! We are put under an obligation that we never can repay in this life or in the life to come. The greatness of this sacrifice cannot be measured, cannot be fully understood by mortal man; but, nevertheless, we can get the benefit of it by faith and obedience to the commandments of God. That is what he requires, and I was going to say how simple it is to keep the commandments of God, and yet it may not be so simple, and it may not be so easy, because *Satan very well knows the mark of our high calling,* and he is seeking continually to lead away the Saints of God from the path of rectitude and from the path of life, *but after all,* my brethren and sisters, *through faith and prayer and diligence, we will surely prevail.*

May the Lord bless us to that end, may he give us a greater and a wider conception of the atonement wrought out by his beloved son. *(CR October 1921, pp.34-36)*

Sacrifice Necessary for Redemption

Charles H. Hart

Elder Hart became a member of the First Quorum of Seventy April, 1906 and served therein until his death in April 1934. He presented the following remarks during October General Conference, 1912.

Spiritual Children of God

We are told, by the Lord: "Behold, this is my work and my glory, to bring to pass the immortality and eternal life of man." We learn in modern revelation of the dignity of the human soul, of its immortality; also that intelligence, an attribute of spirit, "was not created, neither indeed can be," to use the language as recorded in the nineth-third section of the Doctrine and Covenants. We learn that we are the spiritual children of God the Eternal Father. Jesus makes this plain in His answer to Mary, who was first at the sepulchre, when He said, "Touch me not for I have not yet ascended to My Father, but go to My brethren and say unto them, I ascend unto My Father and your Father, to My God and your God." He proclaims there, the Master does, the brotherhood of man and the fatherhood of God; that we are the children, the spiritual children of our Heavenly Father, just as He was the spiritual Son of the Eternal Father. We are told in Psalms that He was the first-born of every creature, meaning of course, the first-born spiritually, because it would not be true that He was the first-born in the flesh of all the children of our Father, or of all the creatures. As He was the spiritual Son of the Eternal Father, so are we the spiritual children of the Eternal Father. *We had a birth before coming to this earth-life.* Element is now added to spirit, and we are told that "spirit and element inseparably connected receiveth a fulness of joy," and this is one of the purposes of our earth-life, that we might have joy. "Adam fell that man might be, and man is that he might have joy," and that he might eventually have immortality and eternal life. There was no lack of appreciation in the value of human life or in the value of a human soul in that the Savior was permitted, as a part of the divine program, to lay down His life for the redemption of mankind.

The Savior's Sacrifice was Indispensible

Some—not of our church and who have not partaken of the light of modern revelation—discuss the question of whether that divine sacrifice might have been dispensed with, and whether it might not have been so ordered by the Father that the earth life of the Son would not have to be sacrificed.

But it was necessary to have the Son lay down His life for the redemption of mankind, to bring about a restoration from the fall that came through Adam. There is significance in the expression of the Savior, "And I, if I am lifted up from the earth will draw all men unto me." It was necessary, no doubt, that He should suffer just as intensely as He did suffer, that His agony should be such that He sweat great drops of blood. That was an unusual occurence. There are only a few recorded instances in the annals of history of men so suffering that they actually sweat blood; but there are a few such instances in addition to that of the Savior where that phenomenon has occurred—men actually sweating blood. Those who hold that it might have been possible, that it might have been just as well for some other program to have been carried out for the redemption of mankind, fail to recognize the fact that God is a God of law and justice. They think because the Father is all-powerful, having the element of omnipotence, that therefore at His will He could have dispensed with the necessity of an atonement; but we must take into account the fact that the Lord is a Lord of justice, of order and of law, as well as a God of mercy, and that mercy can not rob justice.

It is necessary to recognize the harmonies in the attributes of deity. It was by reason of these harmonies existing in the attributes of Deity that it became necessary for the atonement to be made.

(CR October 1912, pp. 15-16)

Christ Suffered Immensely

George F. Richards

This selection is exerpted from Elder Richards' longer sermon to the Saints in General Conference, April, 1937.

Christ Led a Life of Suffering

In the songs that have been composed, as far as my memory serves me, there has been but very little said about the suffering of our Lord during his life up to the time of his betrayal into the hands of his enemies prior to his crucifixion. But as I understand it, brethren and sisters, his whole life, particularly from the time he began his ministry, was one of suffering, intense mental suffering. The bearing of the sins of the world must have been a tremendous load. I think that no mortal man can comprehend it fully, or write it or speak it. We may never know in this life.

Mosiah in the Book of Mormon, tells us that the angel of the Lord talked with King Benjamin and showed him certain things that would take place centruies later, pertaining to the coming forth of our Redeemer, and the atonement. I shall read two or three verses from the third chapter of Mosiah, which tells a wonderful story:

"For behold, the time cometh, and is not far distant, that with power, the Lord Omnipotent who reigneth, who was, and is from all eternity to all eternity, shall come down from heaven among the children of men, and shall dwell in a tabernacle of clay, and shall go forth amongst men, working mighty miracles, such as healing the sick, raising the dead, causing the lame to walk, the blind to receive their sight, and the deaf to hear, and curing all manner of diseases.

"And he shall cast out devils, or the evil spirits which dwell in the hearts of the children of men.

"And lo, he shall suffer temptations, and pain of body, hunger, thirst, and fatigue, even more than man can suffer, except it be unto death; for behold, blood cometh from every pore, so great shall be his anguish for the wickedness and the abominations of his people.

This was fulfilled in the Savior's life as recorded in Luke 22:44, which reads as follows:

"And being in an agony he prayed more earnestly; and his sweat was as it were great drops of blood falling down to the ground."

Jesus Lived and Died For Us

Jesus not only died for his faith and for us but he lived for it, too, and for us he endured mental and bodily pain and anguish of soul beyond the power of mortal man to understand or to endure. The angel told King Benjamin that *the suffering of our Lord as experienced in Gethsemane was due to the wickedness and abominations of the people. This was because he loved them so, his love being perfect.*

Christ Died of a Broken Heart

Elder James E. Talmage, in his book, "Jesus The Christ," tells us that it was his belief that our Savior died from a broken heart. If the wickedness of those for whom he suffered and died was the cause of his extreme suffering, we might ask, how far are we responsible, and what is the measure of our guilt?

Jesus Christ, our Savior, suffered and died for the sins of the world, for those who lived contemporary with him, for those who lived before, and for those who come after, that all men might be redeemed unconditionally from the effects of the Fall of Adam and Eve, from death, through the resurrection.

"For since by man came death by man came also resurrection of the dead, for as in Adam all die, even so in Christ shall all be made alive. (I Cor. 15:21,22)

Also that all mankind might be saved from the effects of their individual sins by obedience to the laws and ordinances of the Gospel. *(CR April 1937, pp.109-110)*

A Sacrifice for Love

Orson F. Whitney

Elder Whitney made these remarks to the members of the Church assembled in General Conference in Salt Lake City, October, 1927.

Because Christ Lives, We Shall Live

Answer now the question: How are the principles of the gospel made available and effectual for man's salvation and exaltation? It is through the Fall and the Redemption. "Adam fell that men might be"—that a race of spirits might tabernacle in the flesh, and thus become souls, capable of endless increase, of eternal progression and exaltation. But the fall brought death—eternal death, which had to be overcome before these spirits, these souls, God's sons and daughters, could fulfill their heaven-decreed destiny and go on to perfection.

Christ overcame death—conquered hell and the grave—died and rose again; *and because he lives we shall live also.* He gained this great victory, not by slaughtering his enemies, but by forgiving them, by allowing his own blood to be shed for them and for all, thus paying a debt that no one else could pay. "Greater love than this hath no man, that he will lay down his life for his friends." But here was One who laid down his life for his enemies as well as his friends. No mere man could do that. It required the love and the life of a God.

He Suffered for All

It took a Being capable of enduring pains that no mere mortal could endure—pains of the body and of the spirit, so terrible, so poignant, so far-reaching and fathomless that the finite mind stands aghast in comtemplation of the infinite and awful mystery; pangs that caused him, "even God, the greatest of all, to tremble because of pain, and to bleed at every pore."

And he "suffered these things for all, that they might not suffer, if they would repent." But if they would not repent, then they must suffer even as did he. (D&C 19:16-18)

"For behold, he suffereth the pains of all men, yea, the pains of every living creature, both men, women and children, who belong to the family of Adam.

"And he suffereth this that the resurrection might pass upon all men, that all might stand before him at the great and judgment day.

"And he commandeth all men that they must repent, and be baptized in his name, having perfect faith in the Holy One of Israel, or they cannot be saved in the kingdom of God.

"And *if they will not repent* and believe in his name, and be baptized in his name, and endure to the end, *they must be damned;* for the Lord God, the Holy One of Israel, has spoken it." (2 Nephi 9:21-24. See also D&C 18:11-12)

Can anyone read that, and believe that all Christ did was to point out the way of Salvation and bid men walk therein? What about the construction of the way? There was no way till he made one. Walking in it, however difficult at times, is a mere bagatelle by comparison.

Adam's Fall Placed Man on Earth

Adam's fall placed man on earth and made available for him the plan of salvation and exaltation. *Without the fall, the spirit would have no body,* and consequently no claim upon the resurrection. And it was Christ who brought about the resurrection. He is its Author. It was his death, his sacrificial offering, that gave vitality to the gospel plan and rendered effectual man's faith and works in his own behalf. Without the Atonement, to offset and nullify the fatal effects of the original transgression, all man's self-help would count for nothing and the very Gospel itself would be mere machinery without the power.

When Adam fell, it was as if the human race had fallen into a pit, from which they were powerless, by any act of their own, to emerge having no means whereby to climb up and out, and not even knowing how to climb. But a Friend, all-wise and all-powerful, comes to the mouth of the pit, compassionates its wretched inmates, and proposes to rescue them from their unhappy situation. He makes of his own life a ladder; lets it down into the pit and says: "Now climb!" They who climb, get out of the pit. They who refuse to climb, remain in the pit—and who is to blame but themselves?

The Crucifixion on Calvary, the self-immolation of a God, is the Rock upon which the gospel rests—the Everlasting Gospel, the ladder unto life eternal.

"Faith without works is dead." We work out our salvation. There is no question about that. *But we work it out through Jesus Christ, and not independently of Him.* We do not save ourselves. We but avail ourselves of the means of salvation provided by our Lord and Savior, the God who died that man might live.

(CR October 1927, pp.147-149)

Symbols of the Atonement

"And he took bread, and gave thanks, and brake it, and gave unto them, saying, This is my body which is given for you: this do in remembrance of me. Likewise also the cup after supper, saying, This cup is the new testament in my blood, which is shed for you."
(Luke 22:19, 20)

Symbols of the Atonement

B. H. Roberts

This explanation is taken from The Seventy's Course in Theology, Fourth Year.

Baptism—A Symbol of the Atonement

The two great Christian institutions of baptism and the sacrament of the Lord's supper have already been alluded to as evidence of the fact of the Atonement. They are now to be considered as symbols of the Atonement. I take up baptism first, as introduced by the Christ himself among the Nephites, because there more perfectly than elsewhere we have this symbol set forth, and only there, in ancient scripture, is the exact formula of the ceremony given. The account of it in the Nephite record stands as follows:

"And he said unto them, on this wise shall ye baptize; and there shall be no disputations among you. Verily I say unto you that whoso repenteth of his sins through your words, and desireth to be baptized in my name, on this wise shall ye baptize them—Behold, ye shall go down and stand in the water, and in my name shall ye baptized them. And now behold, these are the words which ye shall say, calling them by name, saying:

'Having authority given me of Jesus Christ, I baptize you in the name of the Father, and of the Son, and of the Holy Ghost. Amen.'

"And then shall ye immerse them in the water and come forth again out of the water." (3 Nephi 11:22-26)

The Ordinance of Baptism Described

In this ordinance we have recongnized first of all Jesus Christ in whose authority the administrator acts—"Having authority given me of Jesus Christ,"etc. "I baptize you. . .then shall ye immerse them in the water and come forth again out of the water." By this *immersion in the water is symbolized the death and burial of the Christ,* the Atonement he made for the sins of man. *In the coming forth again out of the water, is symbolized the resurrection of the Christ,* his triumph over death, the victory side of the Atonement; death is conquered, life is triumphant; Christ is the first fruits of the resurrection and through him all men participate in the resurrection. "For since by man came death, by man came also the resurrection of the dead. For as in Adam all die, even to in Christ shall all be made alive." (I Cor. 15:21, 22)

Nor is this all; but *in baptism is symbolized the forgiveness of sins* to the baptized. John preached "the baptism of repentance for the remission of sins." (Mark 1:4; Luke 3:3) Peter commanded the multitude on the day of Pentecost to repent and be baptized in the name of Jesus Christ for the remission of sins. (Acts 2:38) "Arise and be baptized and wash away thy sins." (Acts 22:16) "Come unto me and be baptized in my name that ye may receive a remission of your sins." (3 Nephi 30:2) "Thou shalt declare . . . remission of sins by baptism." (D&C 19:31) "Preach repentance and remission of sins by way of baptism in the name of Jesus Christ."

"Know ye not that so many of us as were baptized into Jesus Christ were baptized into his death? Therefore we are buried with him by baptism into death; that like as Christ was raised up from the dead by the glory of the Father, even so we also should walk in newness of life. For if we have been planted together in the likeness of his death, we shall be also in the likeness of his resurrection." (Rom. 6:3-5)

Baptism then not only becomes a symbol of the Christ's death, burial and resurrection to newness of life; but also *the death and burial to sin of the baptized; and his resurrection to righteousness.*

Baptism of the Spirit

Water baptism is completed by the baptism of the spirit, by which man is placed in union with God, through the reception of the

Holy Ghost, foreshadowing that more complete union which shall come when man shall dwell in the very presence of God the Father, and God the Son after the resurrection.

And thus the symbols of the Atonement of Christ to the very uttermost are found in this Christian institution of baptism.

* * *

The Sacrament of the Lord's Supper

[The Sacrament of the Lord's Supper] like baptism, is a permanent Christian institution; and also like baptism it is best set forth in the Nephite scriptures, the Book of Mormon; for there, and nowhere else in ancient scripture, is the formula of the institution as given by the Christ to be found. The prayer of consecration of these symbols is of the highest value, and one of the noblest monuments of Nephite or any other Christian literature extant. I give the prayers of consecration together with the introductory remarks of Moroni which declare their origin.

Sacramental Prayers

Introduction:

"The manner of their Elders and Priests administering the flesh and blood of Christ unto the church. And they administered it according to the commandments of Christ; wherefore we know the manner to be true; and the Elder or Priest did minister it. And they did kneel down with the Church and prayed to the Father in the name of Christ, saying:

Prayer of Consecration over the Broken Bread—the Body:

"O God, the Eternal Father, we ask thee in the name of thy Son Jesus Christ, to bless and sanctify this bread to the souls of all those who partake of it, that they may eat in remembrance of the body of thy Son, and witness unto thee, O God, the Eternal Father, that they are willing to take upon them the name of thy Son, and always remember him, and keep his commandments which he hath given them, that they may always have his spirit to be with them. Amen."

"The manner of administering the wine. Behold they took the cup, and said:

Consecration of the Wine—the Blood:

"O God, the Eternal Father, we ask thee, in the name of thy Son Jesus Christ, to bless and sanctify this wine to the souls of all those drink of it, that they may do it in remembrance of the blood of thy Son, which was shed for them, that they may witness unto thee, O

God, the Eternal Father, that they do always remember him, that they may have his spirit to be with them. Amen." (Moroni 4, 5)

Explanation of the Sacramental Prayers

In these prayers, the whole scheme of man's salvation is a more solemn and awe inspiring title used in addressing the Deity than is used in the Lord's prayer, but that is wholly warranted from the nature of the prayer of consecration which is to follow—"O God, The Eternal Father." And this is repeated in the body of both prayers in a second appeal to God the Father. But this does not fall under the head of "vain repetition," since it is the reptition of emphasis, of deep solemnity, as any one will determine if he considers it with attention and will allow for both the solemnity and greatness of the occasion. But not only is God the Eternal Father recognized in this prayer, but the Son also—"We ask thee in the name of thy Son, Jesus Christ," etc. And not only is the Father and Son recognized but the Holy Spirit also—"That they may always have his spirit to be with them." This prayer of consecration, then, is a confession of faith in the Holy Trinity.

"Bless and sanctify this bread to the souls of all those who partake of it, that they may eat in remembrance of the body of thy Son." . . . "Bless and sanctify this wine to the souls of all those who drink of it, that they may do it in remembrance of the blood of thy Son, which was shed for them." The broken bread is the symbol of the broken or wounded body of the Christ, broken for sinful man. The wine is the symbol of the blood—the blood shed for the sins of men: and the sincere Christian eats of the one and drinks of the other in grateful remembrance of what the Christ has done for him—the suffering he underwent in order to establish justification of man and the forgiveness of his sin under a reign of law, without violence to the Justice of God, or the exclusion of Mercy from our earth-scheme of things. In all this the Atonement is recognized and celebrated most beautifully, and its benefits accepted and appropriated by the celebrants. Moreover, they *witness in the act of eating and drinking these emblems of the body and the blood of the Christ, "that they are willing to take upon them the name," of the Christ,* become "Christians." "And always remember him;" and who could remember him and not with gratitude in view of what he had done for mankind! "And keep his commandments which he hath given them"—a solemn convenant of obedience upon which, as we have seen, depends the reception of the benefits of the Atonement made for man's individual sins—"he [the Christ] became the author of eternal salvation to all them that obey him." And to what end does all this lead—this covenanting to take upon them the name of Christ; to always remember him; to keep his commandments—to what culmination does all this conduct the celebrant? To union with God, the one thing most important; the climax is "that they may always have his spirit to be with them!" Just as the several steps of faith, repentance, and baptism culminate in possession of the Holy Ghost.

Thus in two paragraphs, making less than fifteen lines of printed matter *is given the story of man's redemption,* in this symbol of the Atonement—the Lord's Supper. As in the case of baptism, however, I would remind the student that *the virtue is not in the symbols, but in the realities they represent;* in the actually broken body of Christ—broken by nail-wounds, by crown of thorns, by spear thrusts in the side; by suffering of mental and spiritual agony that made blood-sweat for the body, and torture for the sin-burdened spirit—vicariously suffering for the sins of all men. By these realities was our salvation purchased; and the virtue lies in them, not in the symbols of them. *The symbols we use are in remembrance of the realities, and without mistaking them for the realities themselves.*

(The Seventy's Course in Theology, Fourth Year, 1911, pp. 116-121)

A Sacred Ordinance

Joseph F. Smith

President Smith, before he became a member of the First Presidency of the Church, delivered this message to those gathered in the 13th Ward Assembly Rooms in Salt Lake City, on Sunday, February 9, 1873.

An Important and Sacred Ordinance

The Sacrament of the Lord's Supper is a very important and sacred ordinance; however simple it may appear to our minds it is one which will add to our acceptance before God, or to our condemnation.

It was instituted by the Savior in the place of the law of sacrifice which was given to Adam, and which continued with his children down to the days of Christ, but which was fulfilled in his death, he being the great sacrifice for sin, of which the sacrifices enjoined in the law given to Adam were a similitude.

The Lord designed in the beginning to place before man the knowledge of good and evil, and gave him a commandment to cleave to good and abstain from evil. But if he should fail, he would give to him the law of sacrifice and provide a Savior for him, that he might be brought back again into the presence and favor of God and partake of eternal life with him. This was the plan of redemption chosen and instituted by the almighty before man was placed on the earth. And when man did fall by transgressing the law which was given him, the Lord gave to him the law of sacrifice, and made it clear to his understanding, that it was for the purpose of reminding him of that great event that should transpire in the meridian of time, whereby he and all his posterity might be brought forth by the power of redemption and the resurrection from the dead, and partake of eternal life with God in his kingdom. For this reason Adam and his posterity, from generation to generation, observed this law, and continually looked forward to a time when there should be provided for them a means of redemption from the fall and restoration from death to life, for death was the penalty of the law transgressed, which man was powerless to avert, the fiat of God being, "In the day that thou eatest thereof thou shalt surely die," and this penalty was to follow upon all flesh, all being as helpless and dependent as he was in this matter. Their only hope of redemption from the grave and the power of death was in the Savior whom God had promised, who should suffer death, but being without sin, having himself never transgressed any law, being without blemish, pure and holy, he should have power to break the bands of death and from the grave rise to immortal life, there-by opening the way for all who should follow him in the regeneration to come forth to life again, redeemed from the penalty of the law, and from the sin of transgression to eternal life. In anticipation, therefore, of this great sacrifice which was to be offered for Adam and his seed, they offered sacrifices, more or less acceptably, and in conformity to the pattern given, in proportion to the knowledge of God and of the Gospel which they had, and their faithfulness from generation to generation, to the days of Jesus.

They would take the firstlings of their flocks, the best fruits of their fields, and those things which were emblematic of purity, innocence, and perfection, symbolical of him who was without sin, and as "a lamb slain from the foundation of the world," and offer sacrifices unto God in memory of him, and the matchless and wonderful deliverance to be wrought out for them by him.

* * *

The Law of Sacrifice Fulfilled

When Jesus came and suffered, "the just for the unjust," he that was without sin for him that had sinned, and was subject to the penalty of the law which the sinner had transgressed, the law of sacrifice was fulfilled, and in the stead thereof he gave another law, which we call the "Sacrament of the Lord's Supper," by which his life and mission, his death and resurrection, the great sacrifice he had offered for the redemption of man, should be kept in everlasting remembrance, for said he, "This do in remembrance of me, *for as often as ye eat this bread, and drink of this cup, ye do show the Lord's death till he come."* Therefore this law is to us, what the law of sacrifice was to those who had lived prior to the first coming of the Son of Man, until he shall come again. Therefore we must honor and keep it sacredly, for there is a penalty attached to its violation, as we shall see by reading the words of Paul:

"Wherefore whosoever shall eat this bread and drink this cup of the Lord, unworthily, shall be guilty of the body and blood of the Lord.

"But let a man examine himself, and so let him eat of that bread and drink of that cup.

"For he that eateth and drinketh unworthily, eateth and drinketh damnation to himself, not discerning the Lord's body.

"For this cause many are weak and sickly among you, and many sleep." (I Cor. 11:27-30)

And it is even more plainly given in the Book of Mormon, which I will read.

"And now it came to pass that when Jesus had spoken these words, he turned his eyes again upon the disciples whom he had chosen, and said unto them, behold verily, verily, I say unto you, I give unto you another commandment, and then I must go unto my father, that I may fulfill other commandments which he hath given me. And now behold, this is the commandment which I give unto you, that ye shall not suffer any one knowingly, to partake of my flesh and blood unworthily, when ye shall minister it; For whoso eateth and drinketh my flesh and blood unworthily, eateth and drinketh damnation to his soul: therefore if ye know that a man is unworthy to eat and drink of my flesh and blood, ye shall forbid him." (3 Nephi 18:26-29)

These are some of the injunctions and commandments that are given in relation to the partaking of the Lord's Supper. Now let us be careful what we do, that we may not incur the penalty affixed to the transgression of the law, remembering that *the ordinances which*

God has given are sacred and binding, that his laws are in force, especially upon all that have covenanted with him in baptism, and upon all unto whom they come, whether they embrace them or not, as Jesus said, "This is the condemnation of the world that light has come into the world, but ye love darkness rather than light." Therefore all men will be held accountable for the use they make of the light which they possess. For this reason we are commanded to preach the Gospel unto every creature, that those who obey and are baptized may be saved, and those who reject it may be condemned.

(JD 15:324-5, 327-8)

The Greatest Story in History

"For behold, I, God, have suffered these things for all, that they might not suffer if they would repent." (D&C 19:16)

The Greatest Story in History

Hugh B. Brown

Elder Brown gave us these words in his sermon to April General Conference, 1958.

The Atonement of Christ—A Significant Event

We join with Christians everywhere in commemorating and giving thanks to God for the resurrection of the Lord. The significance of this transcendent event was emphasized by the Apostle Paul in that matchless sermon recorded in Corinthians, in which, among other things, he said: "And if Christ be not risen (from the dead), then is our preaching vain, and your faith is also vain. (I Cor. 15:14)

We believe that the greatest story ever told in all the annals of history is the story of the atonement of Christ. The record of his resurrection and ascension, without which the atonement would not have been complete, is the climax to that story; and now, two thousand years after the event, it is still central and pivotal in all true Christian thought.

Christ was Both Mortal and Divine

Christ was both mortal and divine—mortal through his mother, Mary; divine through his Father, God—and because of that unique combination he was able to yield voluntarily to death in order that through his divinity he might conquer death, break its bands, and make the resurrection possible to all men. The resurrection is not for a select few, nor is it alone for believing Christians; but every man and woman who ever lived upon earth, or who ever shall live thereon, will be raised from the dead.

Paul, the apostle, epitomized the cause and consequences of the atonement in one sentence:". . .as in Adam all die, even so in Christ shall all be made alive." (I Cor. 15:22) And the Savior said,

"Marvel not at this; for the hour is coming in the which all that are in the graves shall hear his voice.

"And shall come forth; they that have done good, unto the resurrection of life; and they that have done evil, unto the resurrection of damnation." (John 5:28-29)

But we must not assume because of this promise that regardless of what we may do we shall have exaltation and eternal life. Those *blessings are reserved for those who accept the gospel of Jesus Christ and observe and keep the commandments of God.*

(CR April 1958, pp. 107-108)

A Wonderful Gift

Joseph Fielding Smith

President Smith delivered this selection to the Saints assembled in General Conference, October, 1947.

Christ Came into the World to Die

May I spend a few minutes presenting before us what we all know to be the truth, that Jesus Christ came into this world to die. That was his mission, and by that death upon the cross and through the shedding of his blood, to bring redemption, twofold, first, to redeem men from Adam's transgression, to restore them again to life, to destory death, gain the victory, which apparently Satan had won through the transgression of Adam. In some manner which I cannot fully explain and which you cannot fully explain, *there was a necessity for an infinite atonement,* a God dying for a fallen world, and that had to be by the shedding of blood, and his blood only could be shed to restore again that life which had been taken away, and bring back again to man the power to live forever. And through his death there comes to us universally, to every living creature, a resurrection of the dead. The Lord does not ask us whether we want to be redeemed from death or not. We were not responsible for it, and, therefore, it is not held against us; it is not to our charge. As Paul has said:

"For as in Adam all die, even so in Christ shall all be made alive." (I Cor. 15:22)

Redemption From Death is a Free Gift

That is the free gift of God the Eternal Father, through Jesus Christ, his Son, to every living soul, men, women, children, from the fall of Adam to the end of time.

Now that is a wonderful gift. It comes without our asking. It comes to the wicked as well as to the righteous. In the fifth chapter of John the Lord speaks to the people of the time coming, and he says it was already here, when the dead should hear the voice of the Son of God and they who heard should live. Yes, not only those who heard it, that is, received his truth, for he added this, when they marveled at what he had to say:

"Marvel not at this: *for the hour is coming, in the which all that are in the graves shall hear his voice.* And shall come forth, they that have done good, unto the resurrection of life; and they that have done evil, unto the resurrection of damnation." (John 5:28, 29)

Here is the word of the Lord himself that he was going to carry the message to the dead; they would all hear; they who were willing to receive that message of truth and abide in it should have everlasting life, but they who would not receive it or who were not worthy to receive it should come forth just the same in the resurrection to receive condemnation, but the resurrection was to come to all universally.

Then again, the Savior died for all men upon the face of the earth, all creatures, that is, human creatures, who were willing to repent of their sins and keep his commandments. He has not redeemed any of us from our sins except it be through repentance and faithful adherence to the principles of the gospel and our endurance to the end.

No Unclean Thing Can Enter His Kingdom

When he stood before his disciples upon this continent, he said to them:

". . .no unclean thing can enter into his kingdom; therefore nothing entereth into his rest save it be those who have washed their garments in my blood, because of their faith, and the repentance of all their sins, and their faithfulness unto the end." (3 Nephi 27:19)

That is definite.

So, he redeemed mankind from death universally, and he has redeemed men from their own sins on conditions of their repentance, and they will not be redeemed from their sins unless they do repent and accept him and wash their garments white in his blood and endure in faith to the end. It is upon those terms that salvation comes.

(CR October 1947, pp.146-147)

Eternal Life—The Greatest Gift

Orson Pratt

This selection is from a sermon delivered by Elder Pratt in the Tabernacle in Salt Lake City on Sunday, September 19, 1880.

Eternal Life versus Eternal Death

Eternal life is said to be the greatest gift of God unto the human family. There are many gifts of God, but this is the greatest of all. In the first place, God has given his Son to die for the human family. What a great gift! *If it had not been for this gift of our Heavenly Father to the inhabitants of our fallen world, the consequence could have been that we should have had eternal death.* What are we to understand by the term eternal death, supposing that there had been no atonement made? What is the meaning of this term? Could you multiply figures enough if you were to take the figures that are now in use and extend them in a line—extend them in a series so that the figures themselves would be as numerous as the particles of the globe—would that express eternal life? Or would it express the duration of eternal death, provided there had been no atonement? No; it cannot be expressed. Hence the atonement of our Savior, which is the gift of God to the fallen inhabitants of this creation, lies at the foundation of all the other gifts given unto the children of men. It is because of this gift that we are permitted to repent of our sins. How could there have been an individual upon all the face of the globe who could have repented, provided there had been no atonement?

Repentance—A Gift of God

Hence you see that repentance is the gift of God, purchased by the atonement. Again, could baptism have been a holy ordinance if it had no saying power in it? Could it have been for the remission of sins, had it not been for the blood of the atonement? No. Baptism, then, is a gift to the children of men as well as repentance. Would the laying on of hands have had any effect upon any person of the human family, in bestowing the gift of the Holy Ghost had there been no atonement? No. Then that is also a gift—the gift of God to man, that his servants should lay their hands upon baptized believers, and that they should be baptized with the Holy Ghost and with fire. Could we have been permitted to partake of the Lord's Supper with any effect whatever? No. Then it is also a gift of God unto man. And thus we may go through all the ordinances, that God ordained from before the foundation of the world unto the present time, and all of them can be called the gifts of God unto man on conditions, and some of them without conditions. The atonement came without any condition on the part of man. It was without repentance, without faith on the part of man. The atonement was something given through the pure love of God to fallen man, without any acts of good works on the part of man. There are some of the blessings, then, that God has ordained for the fallen inhabitants of our globe which come independent of our works, and this is one of which I have been speaking.

All is Vain Without the Atonement

Would there have been any light or intelligence, or goodness or happiness, to be partaken of by fallen man, if it had not been for the atonement? None at all; there could have been no righteousness. But then, all the other gifts that we receive are through works, and by faith and works combined, and it is because of the distinction between these two separate gifts that many of the inhabitants of the earth have erred. Some of them profess to believe that they can obtain all the gifts of God without works, because of some of the sayings of the ancient apostles; while others consider that work must be combined with faith. Now both of these ideas are true when taken in their true light. Eternal life is among all those gifts that are promised of God; such as the gift of repentance, baptism, laying on of hands, etc. All these are not to be compared with the greatness of the gifts called eternal life. I hope that all the Latter-day Saints under the sound of my voice may attain to this, the greatest of all the gifts of God.

(JD 21:312-313)

An Act of Love

B. H. Roberts

During the years of "The Seventy's Course in Theology" the atonement was a popular subject and was discussed numerous times. This selection comes from the course of study for the year 1910.

Evidence of God's Love

I can think of no greater evidence of God's love than that exhibited in the act of permitting his Son, Jesus Christ, to come to the earth and suffer as He did for the sins of the world, that they might not suffer if they would but conform to His laws, and thus accept the terms of salvation. (D&C Section 19) It would seem, too, *that the same attribute of love exists in the breast of the Son, for the sacrifice He made for the redemption of the world was a voluntary act.* He was not compelled to make the Atonement, but of His own free will He volunteered to become our ransom. (Pearl of Great Price) He himself testified: "Therefore doth My Father love me, because I lay down My life, that I might take it again. No man taketh it from Me, but I lay it down of Myself. I have power to lay it down, and I have power to take it again. This commandment have I received of My Father." (John 10:17,18)

Thus, *the atonement of Jesus,* for the children of men, *was a voluntary act;* and His death and suffering for the world, *was the strongest expression of love it is possible to conceive*—"Greater love hath no man than this, that a man lay down his life for his friends." (John 15:13)

(The Seventy's Course in Theology, Third Year, 1910, pp. 186-187)

The Richest Hill on Earth

Charles A. Callis

Elder Callis received the call and was ordained an Apostle, October, 1933 and served faithfully until the time of his death in January, 1947. His remarks here were made ten years earlier, during General Conference, October, 1937.

A Small, Solemn Hill

Butte (Montana) derives its name from the old French word "butte" meaning a rounded hill. The hill is pierced by a hundred shafts from which has been hoisted to the surface $2,500,000,000 of mineral wealth. But values are relative. What men call treasures God calls dross. The truth still remains: "For the love of money is the root of all evil."

When I read that inscription, I said to myself, "There is a small and solemn hill outside the ancient city of Jerusalem which has yielded no mineral treasures, nevertheless it is reverently regarded by true Christians as the richest hill on earth."

Spiritual ruin came by the fall of man. This is the sad story told in the Holy Scriptures: "Because that Adam fell we are; and by his fall came death; and we are made partakers of misery and woe. And men have become carnal, sensual and devilish; and are shut out from the presence of God."

Man, by sin, brought himself into the captivity of sin. His nature by reason of the fall, became evil continually. He was shut out from the presence of the Lord. What a terrible sentence! Imagination cannot conceive a more dreadful judgment. It was not in man's power to escape from the misery that never dies. This judgment mortal man could not reverse. There was no appellate court. It was to be of endless duration. Hope seemed to have bade the world farewell. In despair man stood helpless.

God is Love

Against this dark background, God, who is love and with whom there is forgiveness, caused to shine brightly, the three graces, Faith, Hope and Love. He told Adam that Jesus Christ, the righteous Judge, would come in the meridian of time and atone for original guilt.

Down through the ages this living faith and hope sustained those who believed in the heavenly promises. The Messiah became the consolation of Israel. "God had turned away his judgments because of his Son."

God himself came down from heaven and made the Divine Sacrifice. The God of Nature suffered and died on the Cross. The Apostle Paul said: "We shall be saved by his life, . . . by whom we have now received the atonement. (Romans 5:10)

"The next day John seeth Jesus coming unto him, and saith, behold the Lamb of God, which taketh away the sin of the world." (John 1:29)

Our Savior Paid the Debt

On the Cross our Savior paid the debt that made mankind free. He bought us with the price of his precious blood. We are not our own for we are bought with a price. His blood atones for all our sins, through obedience to righteousness, but it shall not cleanse those who obey not his commandments. The manner of our redemption calls forth our love and affection.

Through the infinite atonement and resurrection of our Lord we receive forgiveness of sin, immortality, a glorious resurrection and eternal life "which gift is the greatest of all the gifts of God" provided we walk before Him, "in all the commandments and ordinances of the Lord blameless." Death lost its sting, the grave its victory. The Savior's death was the door to the glorious resurrection.

Yes, Calvary is the richest hill on earth.

(CR October, 1937, pp. 121-122)

Bibliography

Conference Reports, Salt Lake City, Utah: Deseret News (later Deseret Book), 1880. Not published again until October, 1897. Publishing has since continued twice yearly.

Evening and The Morning Star, The, Independence, Missouri/Kirtland, Ohio: (The Church of Jesus Christ of Latter-day Saints), 1832-1834.

Handbook of the Restoration, Independence, Missouri: Zion's Printing and Publishing Co., 1944.

Journal of Discourses, Volumes 1-26, Liverpool, England: (The Church of Jesus Christ of Latter-day Saints), 1855-1886.

Roberts, Brigham H., *The Seventy's Course in Theology,* Salt Lake City, Utah: for study years 1907, 1908, 1910, 1911, 1912.

Taylor, John, *The Mediation and Atonement,* Salt Lake City, Utah: Deseret News Company, 1882.

Index